1 MONTH OF
FREE
READING

at
www.ForgottenBooks.com

By purchasing this book you are eligible for one month membership to ForgottenBooks.com, giving you unlimited access to our entire collection of over 1,000,000 titles via our web site and mobile apps.

To claim your free month visit:
www.forgottenbooks.com/free892556

ISBN 978-0-265-80799-6
PIBN 10892556

VIEW GARDENS

ELMER E. GOVE
BURLINGTON, VERMONT

1930

DESCRIPTIVE LIST

GLADIOLUS and DELPHINIUMS

Below are some books that everyone having a garden should own. I can take your order and have them sent direct from the publisher.

A Simple Guide to Rock Gardening, by J. L. Cotter. Tells briefly how to build rock, wall, and bog gardens, how to plant, what to plant, and how to care for and cultivate the plants. Written for English conditions but equally valuable in America, as thousands of purchasers will tell you. 126.pp.   **$1.00**

The Standard Cyclopedia of Horticulture, edited by **L.** H. Bailey. This is the one universal and invaluable authority on every horticultural question. Makes a compact but thorough presentation of the kinds, characteristics and methods of cultivation of the plants grown in the United States and Canada for ornament, for fancy, for fruit and for vegetables. Formerly in 6 volumes, but now in three at about half the original price. 5,000 illustrations, 3,637 pages, 3 volumes, fabrikoid binding.
$25.00

The Book of Bulbs, by F. F. Rockwell. Will help you grow bulbs successfully for spring, summer, fall, and winter flowering, inside and outside your home. The information in this book tells, and its pictures show how to grow 70 different bulbous plants including tulips, daffodils, hyacinths, lilies, gladiolus, dahlias, peonies, irises, begonias, cannas, bloodroots, and dozens of others. Recommended as the most complete and newest guide to bulb growing. 187 Ill., 264 pp.   **$3.00**

Dahlias, by F. F. Rockwell. Learn to know the different types of dahlias and their uses in your garden, how to plant and grow them, what fertilizers to use, how to control pests, how to harvest and store the tubers, grow for exhibition, and how to propagate and hybridize. Brief and practical. 65 Ill., 80.   **$1.00**

Gladiolus, by F. F. Rockwell. Recommended as "the best brief guide on gladiolus growing." It tells how to plant, fertilize, and cultivate; how to grow from seed or bulblets; how to harvest and cure; how to handle for cut flowers; and every other detail needed for success with this popular flower. 45 Ill., 79 pp.   **$1.00**

Irises, by F. F. Rockwell. A handy guide which will bring you success with irises and show new uses and effects possible in your garden. Describes the dwarf, early, German, Japanese, Siberian, water, crested, Spanish, English, Dutch and other types; tells the best soils; what fertilizers to use; how to plant; and what care is necessary. Tells how to propagate stock for your own use. 54 Ill., 80 pp.   **$1.00**

The Design of Small Properties, by M. E. Bottomley. Here are 52 carefully designed plans, one or more of which will give you just the planting layout you want for your home. Each plan is fully described and explained so that you can easily modify it to fit any special conditions. A check list of nearly 600 plants showing the height, color, time of bloom, foilage, growing habit, soil requirements, etc., of each one shows you what to plant. 64 Ill., 233 pp.   **$3.00**

How to Grow Fine Flowers, by E. H. and R. T. Wilson. A very fine 212 page book for amateurs. It is written by practical men who actually run a popular garden themselves. The book treats of a great many subjects. Also contains a pronunciation dictionary and germination table.   **$2.50**

FOREWORD

To those who have grown the gladiolus there is no need to speak about the good qualities of this wonderful flower. They know. But as thousands of people will get this catalog who have never grown any "glads" or perhaps only a few of the older varieties I want to say a few words to them. There are thousands of other flowers suitable for your garden, all beautiful and all having their places in the general scheme of things. But there is none that will give you the same amount of pleasure and beauty and all-round satisfaction as the gladiolus. There is no other flower that has the almost infinite variety of color and form as the gladiolus. Colors range thro almost every conceivable shade and new colors and shades and forms are being introduced every year.

There is a fascination about growing glads that becomes a hobby, then a craze. There are five stages of interest in growing "glads". First you just grow them as an amateur, same as you would any other flower. Then as your interest in them increases you become a "fan", then a "bug", then a "nut" and finally a "fiend." When you reach this final stage you are hopeless. You think of "glads" all day, dream of them at night, spend every available minute of your time in the garden, talk of them, visit the shows, read all the catalogs and spend all your money on them. You will look lovingly at the last flower in the fall, will handle over your bulbs in the winter time and will hardly be able to wait till you can lovingly plant the bulbs in the spring. From then till the first bloom appears is a period of happy anticipation. When finally the spikes of bloom begin to appear you are in heaven.

And why isn't this as well as to play golf? Personally I would like to play golf if I had the time but I don't believe any golf enthusiast ever got more fun out of the game then the rabid "glad fiend" gets out of growing glads.

USES OF THE GLADIOLUS. Aside from a few varieties that are especially adapted for landscape planting, the gladiolus is preeminently valuable as a cut flower. Some varieties are valuable for planting in a group to make a mass effect of a certain color. But as a rule they do not make a pleasing effect in the garden unless the old faded flowers are kept picked off.

The greatest use of the gladiolus is as a cut flower and it is used for every conceivable purpose for which cut flowers are used. Millions are raised every year for the florist trade to be used in wedding decorations, funeral work, table decorations, baskets, bridal bouquets, etc. But the florists do not use enough of the newer and better varieties. To them a glad is a glad. They should help educate the public to the newer and more beautiful varieties.

For the home they help to brighten things up with their beautiful colors. Any color scheme can be created by using the right varieties. The tips of the prim varieties are beautiful for table bowls. By using the right varieties you can have any conceivable arrangement of bloom from the most dainty to the most majestic.

CULTURE. The culture of the gladiolus is about as easy as anything can be. They grow in any kind of soil from the lightest sand to heavy clay. And they **do not** want rich soil, at least no manure near the bulbs. Just plant them four to six inches deep, keep the weeds out, and in dry weather water them if necessary. With every order I enclose detailed directions for growing them. But remember it is easy to have wonderfully fine flowers and they require no special care.

Tho glads will do well most everywhere except in the shade and will give you good results under adverse conditions, they will respond to good treatment and repay you bountifully for any extra care you give them. Some varieties will respond more than others to special care. Like any other plant you can't expect to get the same results if you plant them in dry sand or hard clay and do not give them water. They like lots of water but do not want wet feet. That is, they must have good drainage, If water stands on the land they will not do nearly as well as they will where the water drains off. If your soil is very dry they will appreciate a good thorough watering once a week or so. They **will bloom** under adverse conditions but will be much better under more favorable soil conditions. They are not at all fussy but like other plants will respond to ordinary sense in their culture.

BLOOMING DATES. I cannot give the blooming dates of the various varieties. For one reason I seldom plant large bulbs and of course it takes longer for the small sizes to come to bloom.

Secondly, when exact dates are given it is often misleading. The same variety varies greatly under different conditions. Late planted ones will not bloom much later than the early planted ones. If 100 bulbs of the same size of most any one variety are planted at one time, they will probably come into bloom over a period of at least a month.

I can only tell if a variety is early, midseason or late with some qualifications as to extra early or late. This is the best I can do.

TO GET THE MOST out of your glads you should have them bloom thro as long a season as possible. Get some very early ones and some of the late ones. You will appreciate these even more than those that bloom thro the middle of the season. Cara Mia is the earliest variety I grow and Salmon Glow comes next, then Apricot Glow and Quinton. You should have some of these. There are several late ones. W. H. Phipps, Herbstzauber, Indian Summer, Mrs. Peters, Lorice are fine late ones.

WHAT IS THE BEST GLAD in a certain color? Or the best 10? There is no best one for all purposes. Some do well in some places and not so well in others. A variety that might be fine for exhibition might be entirely out of place in a bridal bouquet. Then two varieties of nearly the same color but of different seasons of blooming may both be good and should have a place in your garden. There is no use or sense in comparing Gold Eagle with Golden Dream or Mary Frey with Mrs. Peters or Apricot Glow with Richard Diener. The first named ones are nearly thro blooming before the others begin to bloom. You need both the early and the late ones and some in between.

A variety that you may think is the ultimate of perfection another person may not like at all. And so it goes. Try out the various varieties and save the ones you like best.

QUALITY OF BULBS. I think it is generally considered that northern grown bulbs are the best. The cool climate gives them a vigor that southern grown bulbs do not have as a rule. While I do not claim that we grow better bulbs than anyone else I have often found that new varieties that I buy do better the second season from the bulbs I grow here than they did from the original bulbs. I have many letters from customers who say my bulbs have given very fine results. I always disinfect my bulbs before planting and plant on new land every year; which is necessary if the health and vigor of the bulb is maintained. My bulbs this year are the finest and cleanest I have ever grown.

GUARANTEE. Every bulb is guaranteed to be true to name and healthy. We are all human and so subject to mistakes and occasionally a bulb gets by that is not right. But in that case don't tell your neighbors but tell me and I will adjust the matter to your entire satisfaction. In fact, **I guarantee satisfaction.**

I am not only trying to sell bulbs but also make steady customers. My enemies (and I probably have some) won't buy of me anyway. The only people to whom I can sell the second order are my friends, so I am going to try to make you a friend if you will give me a chance.

The growers as a whole are a fine bunch of fellows and try to do the right thing. But there are some who are not so careful as they should be. It is no small job to grow several hundred varieties and keep them all absolutely true to name and to send out only good healthy bulbs. It requires eternal vigilance and personal supervision to have everything satisfactory to the customer. But this is what I try to do, in fact, **guarantee to give satisfaction.** My bulbs this year are the finest I ever had.

I have grown and sold bulbs for the past seven years and every year my business has increased at least fifty per cent. The past year it was nearly sixty per cent. Judging from the way the orders have come in before this catalog was published, the increase this year will be much larger than ever before. This would seem to indicate that I please my customers.

ORDER EARLY. There is everything to gain and nothing to lose by ordering early. If you wait there is the possibility and in some varieties the strong probability of their being sold out long before spring. Some varieties are always sold out early and we can't tell beforehand just which ones they are going to be. Sometimes a grower will think a certain variety is especially good and will pick up all he can find. Or else the public will want a variety in quantity before there is stock enough to go round.

In fact before this catalog was in print I was sold out of some sizes in several varieties.

Then if you wait till spring as many do, we are always rushed with orders at that time and can't give the individual attention to them that we can if we have the orders earlier in the season.

If you do not want to spend all your money early in the season you can send on the order with a deposit of 25% and I will hold it till March 15th. But when the full amount is sent with the order I am more generous with extras.

ABOUT SIZES. As you will see in the price list the bulbs are listed in six sizes. If you want the very best blooms get No. 1. As a rule these will produce the biggest spikes and blooms. The smaller the bulb the smaller the plant and bloom. No. 3 will give fine blooms in most varieties. Even No. 4 will produce good blooms in many varieties and Nos. 5 and 6 will bloom in some varieties but will be much smaller. If you are growing for increase, get Nos. 4,, 5 or 6. These are all grown from bulblets and will produce more bulblets than older bulbs as a rule. Generally bulbs two years old from bulblets are considered the best for bloom. That is what Nos. 1, 2 and 3 usually are

BULBLETS. For those who can't afford to buy high priced bulbs and are willing to wait a year or two and want to "grow their own" so as to get them cheaper a good way is to buy bulblets. Occasionally a variety will bloom from bulblets the first year but it usually takes two years to get a good bloom. But I want it distinctly understood that I **do not** replace bulblets if they do not grow. The bulblets of some varieties nearly all grow but in most kinds you cannot depend on more than 75 or 80% and in some kinds it takes expert treatment to make any germinate. So that if you buy one or two high priced bulblets of any variety and they do not grow it is your loss. Different conditions also have a great deal to do with the germination of bulblets. You would probably have good luck growing them but you have to take your chances the same as I do.

PRICES, TERMS, ETC. Unfortunately there are all kinds of prices in this gladiolus business. Often growers just starting in think they have got to sell cheap in order to sell at all and they do but usually their stock is very small so that their prices should not effect prices in general. It is part of my business to keep track of prices and if I find well known reliable growers are selling for less than I am I will put in extra bulbs to make up the difference. Don't hesitate about prices. Just send in your orders and I will see that you get your money's worth. Then it is worth a little more to get bulbs from a grower who you know produces good stock and is willing and eager to make things right if anything should turn out wrong.

I cannot accept orders for less than $1.00. I lose money on orders of less than $1.00, in fact make very little on orders of less than $2.00; not enough to pay for the bother. But I know that a lot of beginners don't want to spend so much so will accept orders for $1.00. But just wait till these beginners get the "Glad Bug." Then is when I make my money.

EXTRAS ON ORDERS. On **cash** orders of $2.00 to $5.00 you can select 5% extra in bulbs of your own choosing, $5.00 to $25.00 you can select 10%, $25.00 to $50.00 15% and $50.00 to $100.00, and over, 20% extra.

These orders must include at least three varieties and are not for quantities priced by the 1,000. Also does not include the variety "Inspiration" or mixtures.

On cash orders of $10.00 or more for bulbs priced per each and per 10 I will give a copy of the Gladiolus book by Rockwell if you ask for it. This is a very good book on the growing of gladiolus.

In addition to the above I usually slip in something extra that I think will please you. If there is some variety that you are interested in just mention it and if the price is not too high and if I have stock enough I will put in a bulb of it. I like to be generous in filling orders.

MIXTURES. I do not advise an advanced amateur ever to buy a mixture of glads. And they usually will not. It is so much more fun to keep the kinds separate and learn to know them all by name, learn the different characteristics of the various varieties. Then if there is one you especially like and you want to get more you know what it is you want.

But there are thousands of people who have gardens, who want a few glads and have not yet got the "bug" and so do not want to bother with keeping the kinds separate. For these people I have a mixture that is especially good. It contains at least thirty varieties, good ones in many different shades. These are mixed as the orders come in, so if you prefer more of one shade and less of others I can mix them that way. If you do not like reds I can leave them out and the same with other colors. If you leave it to me I will give you a fine assortment of at least thirty kinds in the collections of 50 or more bulbs. Bulbs are at least 1 inch in diameter and not the little ½ inch bulbs put out in many collections.

THIS IS MY NO. 1 COLLECTION.

They are priced at $3.00 for 100 bulbs, prepaid. $1.75 for 50 or $1.00 for 25, all prepaid. Next fall if you want your money back just say so. **I don't believe there is as good a mixture offered by any other grower in the country at anywhere near the price.**

I have had many wonderful reports from the collections I sent out last year.

I also have a **NO. 2 COLLECTION** at the same price. This includes only prim- ulinus varieties.

NO. 3 COLLECTION $5.00 per 100, 50 and 25 at the 100 rate. This includes at least 40 varieties in many different shades and several of the newer varieties.

NO. 4 COLLECTION $10.00 per 100, 50 and 25 at the 100 rate. This contains at least 50 varieties including many of the finest exhibition varieties and is sure to please anyone. If labeled these collections would cost a great deal more.

Certain varieties are included in all the mixtures but in the higher priced ones are some varieties that are exceptionally fine and of an exhibition quality. All are very well worth the money. I am not afraid to compare them with any collection in the country.

But remember the varieties in the collections are not labeled.

PRONUNCIATION OF GLADIOLUS. At the annual meeting in Rochester, New York in 1925 of the American Gladiolus Society, the members went on record as favoring the pronunciation of glad-i-o'-lus and using the one form for both singular and plural. Now let's all work for this one pronunciation and tell our friends about it and do away with the confusion that has existed before in regard to this word.

AMERICAN GLADIOLUS SOCIETY

or **A. G. S.** for short. This is the fastest growing special flower society in the world. It has about 5,000 members now, all of whom are working for the advancement of the gladiolus. We need your help too. The dues are $2. a year for which you get the sat- isfaction of helping along the good cause and you also get "THE GLADIOLUS REVIEW," a monthly magazine devoted solely to the gladiolus. This magazine is worth much more than $2.00. You will also get other literature and catalogs. Send me the $2.00 and I will see that you are enrolled as a member, and will give you a large bulb each of Golden Frills and Copper Bronze free. This is for new members only, not for trans- fers in the same family. Use the coupon in the back of this catalog.

THE FLOWER GROWER

is the name of a first class monthly magazine devoted to flowers, nature, birds, bees' etc. Fine editorials. One of the very best. $2.00 a year. Address Madison Cooper' Calcium, N. Y.

INTRODUCING

Inspiration

(E. F. PALMER)

Five years ago the Kiwanis Club of Barrie, Ontario offered a silver cup to the Canadian Gladiolus Society to be awarded to the best seedling gladiolus shown at their annual show with the provision that the seedling must be of outstanding merit to receive the award. The winning seedling was to receive the name Kiwanis. No award was made that year nor since till this past year 1929 tho the competition has been very keen. No seedling was shown in the 4 years previous to 1929 that the judges considered good enough to receive a name like Kiwanis, which is the name of one of the very best service clubs and known throughout the world.

But at the show held in Barrie in 1929, Mr. E. F. Palmer of Vineland, Ontario, showed three spikes of a beautiful pink which four leading disinterested judges unanimously agreed was worthy of the Kiwanis award. It was a very beautiful and absolutely distinct variety and surely deserved the prize. It was duly named Kiwanis, the cup was given to Mr. Palmer and it had a good start on a glorious career.

But three months after the show Mr. Palmer received notice from Kiwanis headquarters that they would not allow their name to be used in any such way. So it was necessary to rename it and the name "Inspiration" was chosen. This name means something to Mr. Palmer as it was the first outstanding seedling he produced and was an inspiration to him to continue his efforts in hybridizing, work which is being rewarded by a wonderful lot of seedlings coming along, several of which you will hear from later when he has worked up a stock of them. (Apricot Glow is not a product of Mr. Palmer's own hybridizing tho he introduced it.)

Here is Mr. Palmer's description of Inspiration:

"Inspiration" (25241, Dr. Bennett x Gloriana). Deep shrimp pink (Ridgeway) self color except for very light flecking of peach red at edges of petals. Throat lightly marked with light mauve feathering on creamy pink ground, diffused. Bloom form is unusual and very fine, the petals being waved, fluted, semi-lacinated, giving a very pleasing and highly decorative effect. Blooms are Dr. Bennett size, wide open, heavy texture and withstands heat exceptionally well. 7-8 out on spikes from No. 1 bulbs. 4-5 out from No. 3 and No. 4 bulbs. From very large bulbs the first 3 or 4 blooms to open are inclined to "lily" form and face upwards. Blooms from all size bulbs open perfectly as a cut flower and maintain size well to tip blooms. Tall strong grower, robust plant, moderate propagator, making 40 to 50 cormels per bulb and germinating 75%. 85-90 days to bloom.

I have made a deal with Mr. Palmer to introduce "INSPIRATION." I am trying to find outstanding varieties to introduce but positively will not boost a variety that is not top-notch and distinctive and worthy of a place along with the best already on the market. There are a great many varieties introduced every year that never should go outside their originator's gardens. Probably I have been stung as many times as the next man by inferior introductions. I realize that no person can always pick the good ones but I do surely feel that "INSPIRATION" is a variety that will make a name for itself without any special boosting.

"INSPIRATION" should not be introduced this year as the stock is very limited but Mr. Palmer has 2 or 3 others that will be ready to introduce next year so we decided to put it out this year at the very moderate price of $10.00 each for any size bulb. We have already sold quite a few so if you want bulbs larger than No. 4 you had better get your order in early.

$10.00 EACH, 12 FOR $100.00

Emile Aubrun

Annie Laurie

Aflame

6

Lorice

Jean du Tailles

Iwa

Golden Dream

(K) means Kunderd the originator; (Pf.) Pfitzer; (Horn) Hornberger; (Kirch) Kirchoff.

A. B. KUNDERD. (K) Cream, tinted pink, cerise lines on light yellow lip. Very heavily ruffled and beautiful. Good size.

A. E. KUNDERD. (K) Very large. Salmon pink with rose red blotch. Heavily ruffled . Called a glorified Marshall Foch.

ALBATROSS. (Pf.) Very large pure white. Several blooms open. One of the very finest whites.

AL SMITH. (K) New tall Salmon rose.

AMBROSIA. (K) Old rose of a beautiful new shade.

AMETHYST. (Errey) Deep lavender with deeper throat blotch. Ruffled. Opens 8-10 well placed blooms. A very beautiful variety and bound to be popular.

ANGEL'S DREAM. (Ellis) Large light pink. Many open. Fine.

ANNA EBERIUS. (D) Very popular violet purple.

ANNIE LAURIE. (Brown) Heavily ruffled delicate pink overlaid with light rose pink. Light purplish lines in the throat. 4-6 medium sized distinctive shape blooms open at a time. Good height, strong grower, fine propagator. This is one of the most exquisitely beautiful Glads in existence. A Glad that has a character that sets it apart from other Glads. Annie Laurie is not only a very beautiful Glad for the home garden but will become immensely popular as a commercial variety. I have very strong recommendations from some of the leading florists of the country and from many amateurs. You must see it to appreciate it.

I have the largest stock in the country and can furnish any amount in most sizes.

ANTHONY ZONKER. (K) Dark salmon with beautiful velvety red blotch. Large, ruffled. 5-8 or more open.

ANTIONE. (K) Clear very deep ruffled yellow. Medium size but fine.

ANTONIA ANTONETTE. (K) Soft salmon rose, large. Several open. Long spike.

AVE MARIA. (Pf.) Large flowering light blue with small purple blotches. 7-8 open. Fine.

BENGAL TIGER. (Pratt) Large oriental red with almost black stripes. Odd but pretty. Very popular.

BERTIE SNOW. (Mair) Pinkish lavender. Large flowers well placed on long spike. A magnificient varety when it comes clear. Sometimes flecks. Some growers consider this is the finest lavender. Great exibition variety. Good propagator.

BETTY NUTHALL. (Salbach) Warm coral pink with pale orange throat markings. Several large well placed flowers open. Wonderfully strong grower. Late. This is one of the very finest pinks on the market. Bound to be extremely popular both with amateurs and commercial growers.

BLANCHE BOLLINGER. (K) Ruffled old rose striped lighter.

BLEEDING HEART. (Brown) Light pink with large red blotch. Somewhat similar in color to Pendleton but colors more contrasty. Tall spike with 8-10 large perfectly placed blooms open. Very strong grower. Was scored 98 at the Boston Show. Fine exhibition variety.

BLUE TORCH. (Horn) Light blue somewhat similar to Rev. Ewbank but little lighter in color, larger flower, and a straight spike. Several open. Good commercial.

BLUSHES OF CREAM. (K) Light creamy pink, canary yellow throat. Several open. One of the best varieties Kundred put out last year.

BOBBY. (K) Large deep rose with purplish red blotch. Fine.

BREAK O'DAY. (Bill) Large early light pink. Very popular.

BRIDAL VEIL. (Austin) Ruffled white with greenish buds. Several well placed blooms open. This has been very fine this past year. Distinctive.

8

BYRON L. SMITH. (K) Pale lavender pink or pinkish lavender, cream throat. 8 or more blooms open. Fine variety when well grown.

CABERNET. (Metzner) Bluish wine color. A fine "Smoky". Odd and distinct color.

CALIFORNIA. (Kirch) Orange. Very large blooms on tall strong growing plant. Admired by everyone who likes orange. One of the best.

CANBERRA. (Errey) Very tall plant, long spikes of clear yellow, buds greenish. Some consider this the finest exhibition yellow. It's only fault is that the blooms often come in two rows faced too far apart. Fair propagator.

CAPT. BOYNTON. (Boynton) Lavender blue on white ground, purplish blotch on lower petals. Tall straight plant. Large wide open flowers. Good commercial and popular.

CARDINAL PRINCE. (K) Clear cardinal red. Several well placed blooms open. Strong grower and propagator. One of the best reds..

CAROLUS CLUSIUS. (Velthuys) The light pink of a "different" shade. Light rose or deep shrimp pink. Several large blooms open. Very fine grower and propagator. The first time I imported this I liked it so well I imported more the next year. Will become a fine commercial. You better try it.

CATHERINE COLEMAN. (C) Clear salmon rose with purplish pencilings on lower petals. Several large well placed flowers open at a time on tall straight spike. One of the very best.

CATTLEYA ROSE. (K) Large flower of an orchid rose shade different from any other. Creamy yellow on lower petals. Ruffled.

CHAS. F. FAIRBANKS. (K) Popular light red. Garden visitors always admire it.

CHERRY ROSE. (K) Large cherry red flowers on tall, strong plant. Lower petals feathered with darker rose and creamy lines. Distinct and very well liked.

CHICAGO. (K) Heavily ruffled deep pink with darker blotch. Bluish line around all petals. Several open.

COLOR MARVEL. (K) Deep vermillion, lower petals darker. Velvety appearance. This is a distinctly beautiful variety and must be seen to be appreciated.

CORONADO. (Briggs) Extremely large ruffled white with purple feather in the throat. Scarce.

CORYPHEE. (Pf.) Very large light pink with white throat. Several open. A fine one and in big demand.

CRIMSON GLOW. (Betscher) Large crimson. An old standard variety and still one of the best.

CRINKLES. (K) Heavily ruffled dark pink. One of the oldest ruffled varieties and still going strong.

DESDEMONE. (Vilmorin) Smoky purple, cream center. Large blooms, strong grower. One of the very best smokies. Very fine.

DOMINUS. (K) Very deep purplish red with darker throat blotches. Several well placed blooms open at a time.

DORCAS ALDRICH. (Dusinberre) Rose pink overlaid with ashes of roses. Several blooms open. Tall and fine. Early.

DORRITT. (K) Large light lavender pink often flaked darker lavender. Velvety red lines in throat. Several open. Well liked when it comes clear and when flaked.

DR. CHRIST MARTZ. (K) Large ruffled light red. Very good.

DR. F. E. BENNETT. (D) Fiery scarlet. Several very large well placed blooms open. Strong grower. The best glad in its color.

DR. L. H. BAILEY. (K) Deep tyrian rose with deeper red blotches. The whole flower has a velvety appearance that I have never seen in any other variety. Several open. Very pretty.

DR. MOODY. (Kinyon) Light lavender sometimes flaked darker. Very pretty either way. 8 or more blooms open. Very strong grower and propagator. One of the very best lavenders. Fine for exhibition and will be a good commercial. Garden visitors always like it. Fairly early.

DR. NELSON SHOOK. (K) Deep tyrian rose, somewhat like Taro but little lighter and even stronger grower. Large strong spikes with several blooms open. One of the best varieties on the market.

DR. STARKWEATHER. (K) Deep lavender rose with "Pendleton" blotches. Tall strong grower.

DR. W. VAN FLEET. (K) Bright rose pink shading to cream yellow throat. Tall straight plant. Very early. Good commercial.

DUCHESS OF YORK. (Pf.) Tall bluish purple, 8-10 well placed blooms open. Always sells well.

PHIPPS. (Ellis) Somewhat similar to Phipps but smaller and much earlier **EARLY**

ED. SPRINGER. (K) Light lavender rose pink splashed with darker markings.

E. G. HILL. (K) A true pink with cream throat. Several perfectly placed blooms open. Very good.

EIGHTH WONDER. (K) Deep smoky old rose. Very large flowers and very strong, heavy foilage. Very fine variety. Late.

ELF. (D) White, lemon lip. 6-8 blooms open at a time on tall strong plant. Fine commercial. One of the best whites.

ELLA DAY. (Carpenter). Immense La France pink with red lines on pale yellow blotch. Fine.

ELROSE. (K) Very pale pink flaked deeper. Cherry red blotch. General effect is pink and white striped.

EMILE AUBURN. (Lemoine) Coppery bronze sometimes overlaid with slate. Large cherry red blotch. Many large perfectly placed blooms open at one time. One of my customers had a spike with 24 buds and 12 open at once. When well grown this is magnificent. Very outstanding. Fine propagator. Everyone should have this.

ENSIGN. (Errey) Large bright red with white blotch. Very showy. Strong grower.

EUGENE LEFEBVRE. (Lemoine) Bright rose pink blotched amaranth and cream. Several well placed blooms open. Very well liked.

EXCELLENCE. (K) Light red, practically a self color. Large flowers. Tall plant. Very showy. Fine.

FAITH. (Kinyon) The new light blue that has been greatly admired.

FAY LAMPHIER. Immense soft rose pink. This is universally admired by visitors to the garden. Customers write me that I do not say enough about it in my catalog, that there is nothing else like it. Fine grower. You better try it.

FERN KYLE. (K) Very large ruffled cream white. Strong grower, a fine seller.

FIRE GLOW. (K) Clear vivid glowing scarlet.

FIRE PINK. (K) Deep salmon red, practically a self color.

FONTAINE. (Coleman) Beautiful ruffled peaches and cream. Long spike. Fine grower and propagator. Great florist variety. Every florist can use this variety.

FRANK J. SYMMES. (D) Ruffled dark salmon. Tall strong grower. Very nice variety.

FULD'S FAVORITE. (K) Very beatuiful light lavender rose. Several open. One of the best.

GAY HUSSAR. (Salbach) Seedling of Nancy Hanks which it resembles somewhat but has brighter colors. Salmon orange, shading to yellow throat with scarlet throat markings. Several large perfectly placed blooms open at a time. A very fine showy glad. Sure to please.

GENE STRATTON PORTER. (K) Delicate soft pink. Late.

GERALDINE FARRAR. (D) Lavender blue. The color is distinct and one of the best light blues. When first introduced this variety did not seem very strong but the past two years has been very good.

GERTRUDE ERREY. (Errey) Medium bright pink at edge shading to nearly white in the throat which is marked with a crimson feather. A tinge of glistening salmon lights up the whole flower making it very attractive. 6-10 perfectly placed blooms are open at a time. Tall and straight.

10

GERTRUDE PFITZER. (Pf.) Light blue, larger than Mrs. Konynenburg. Several open. Tall straight plant. Fine.

GIANT NYMPH. (Coleman) Very large light salmon rose. Tall strong grower. One of the best commercials.

GLORIANA. (Betscher) Golden salmon, clear yellow throat. To me this has about the most beautiful color I have ever seen in a gladiolus. Several open. Tall slender plant. Fine propagator. Fine commercial.

GLORY OF THE U. S. A. (Cary) Rich orange salmon edged and veined with scarlet blending to flush salmon. Apricot and cream throat. Lower petals of lemon yellow with red lines. Large flowers. Very tall strong healthy plant. One of the best of the new varieties. I think it will become popular when known.

GOLD. (Decorah) Clear yellow. Several open. Has been one of the leading yellows.

GOLD EAGLE. (Austin) Deep yellow clear. Slightly ruffled. Extremely early and valuable on that account. Wonderful propagator.

GOLDEN BROWN. (K) The nearest to a brown I have seen. Ruffled. Very distinctive color and pretty. Sure to become popular.

GOLDEN DREAM. (Groff) Very beautiful absolutely clear deep yet soft yellow that is distinctive from any other. Several good sized blooms open at a time. Very tall, straight, strong growing plant. An outstanding variety that will be in demand for years. One of the 2 or 3 best yellows on the market and by far the best that can be had in quantity. Many customers have written me of the wonderful beauty of this variety. Midseason to late.

GOLDEN MEASURE. (Kelway) Deep yellow but not so dark or clear as Golden Dream. Tall grower. Heavy spike with several blooms open. The best of the cheaper yellows.

GOLDEN SALMON. (K) Very large beautiful golden salmon color. Popular.

GOLDEN SNAPDRAGON. (K) A new type, heavily ruffled. Upper petals cream, lower ones yellow. Snapdragon shape. Pretty. Very early.

GORGEOUS. (K) Beautiful rose red with velvety red throat blotch. Very showy and beautiful.

GRACE KIMBALL. (Decorah) Pale violet with darker blotch. A good blue but slow propagator.

GRAND GUARDIAN. (Austin) Mrs. Austin's new yellow which she considers her best. Deep yellow with soft rose feather in throat which gives the whole flower a darker shade. Large ruffled blooms. Several open. Tall strong plant but not so long spike of bloom as I would like.

HAMBURG PINK. (Hornberger) Very large bright pink. Good.

HEAVENLY BLUE. (PF) Pale sky blue with few darker lines in the throat. 8-10 good sized perfectly placed blooms open. The finest light blue in existence. This is good.

HEINRICH KANZLEITER. (Pf.) An early dark velvety red. A good one.

HELEN HOWARD. (Austin) Bronzy buff with amber yellow throat. Several well placed blooms open. Tall and straight. The best in its color.

HELEN PHIPPS. (Diener) Somewhat similar to W. H. Phipps but darker rose color and much better propagator. Late.

HELEN WILLS. (Salbach) Tall large white with pale lemon throat. Several open. Looks like a fine commercial.

HENRY C. GOEHL. (Fischer) Large white, slightly flushed pink. Crimson blotch on lower petals. Very popular.

HERBERT HOOVER. (K) Tall plant, deep cherry rose. Somewhat like Pendleton.

HERBSTZAUBER. (Pf.) Large orange salmon much like Pfitzer's Triumph but without the dark blotch. Tall, late. Very good.

HIGHLAND LADDIE. (K) Light rose pink. Very popular.

HIGH NYE. (Austin) It sure is high, about the tallest glad I ever saw. Long, slender spike. Old rose with cream throat. Several open. Fine for large baskets. Great propagator.

IMPRESSARIO. (K) Kundred's largest and best lacinated variety. Clear lemon yellow. Really very fine.

INDIAN CHIEF. (K) Very large deep purplish red. This is fine and I think will be very popular when known.

INDIAN SUMMER. (K) Large massive lavender. Very heavy spike and plant. One of the most beautiful varieties in existence but very late and not so good as a propagator.

IVER'L. (AUSTIN) Mrs. Austin's new white. Pure white even to the pollen. Large and good.

IWA. (BETSCHER) Light rose, red blotch. Several open. A fine variety but you need at least a No. 4 bulb to be sure of bloom.

JACELIA. (K) Deep rose pink. Several open. Good.

JACOBA V. BEIJEREN. (HEEMSKERK) J. V. B. for short. Light purple self color. Many open. Beautiful.

JANE ADDAMS. (DECORAH) Immense soft phlox pink with white throat. Really a light lavender. Very fine.

JAP LADY. (DECORAH) Beautiful distinct shade of light purple with darker blotch. Very distinct and beautiful.

JEAN DU TAILLIS. (LEMOINE) Large spike of beautiful blotched pink. One of the best blotched varieties.

JENNY LIND. (DECORAH) Clear light salmon, cream throat. Several open One of the finest pinks, great commercial. I have a strain of this that is much stronger and gives better spikes than the ordinary strain on the market.

J. H. McFARLAND. (K) Light bronze. Very tall but short spike of bloom.

JOERG'S WHITE. (JOERG) Immense cream white. Makes a great spike. Good seller but rather slow propagator.

J. OGDEN ARMOUR. (K) Rose salmon, buds are orange. Dark red blotch. Ruffled. Very pretty.

JONKHEER VAN TETS. (PF.) Very large pure white. Several open. Very fine.

JOHN T. McCUTCHEON. (K) Very fine large red somewhat similar in color to Bobby tho' distinct.

JOHN T. PIRIE. (K) Mahogany brown with darker throat bordered yellow. Very distinct and odd, yet beautiful.

KING GEORGE. (MAIR) Large red with white throat. Several open. Tall strong plant.

KING OF REDS. (K) Large red with darker markings.

KING TUT. (DAVIS) Large light salmon rose finely splashed darker. Very tall strong plant with large spike of bloom.

KIRCHHOFF'S APPLE BLOSSOM. (KIRCHHOFF) Beautiful pink and cream.

KIRCHHOFF'S VIOLET. (KIRCHHOFF) Real violet blue. A good one and in big demand. Several open.

KUNDERD'S APPLE BLOSSOM. (K) Dainty Apple Blossom color.

KUNDERD'S YELLOW FAVORITE. (K) Very deep yellow. Soft red inconspicuous lines in the throat.

KUNDERD'S YELLOW WONDER. (K) Large clear yellow. Several open. Midseason.

LACINATUS. (K) Small rose pink. Petals are cut or lacinated on the edges. Said to be valuable in hybridizing and as a forcer in the greenhouse.

LAIDLEY. (ERREY) Pale pink, nearly white, streaked with darker shades of pink. Cream band on lower petals, crimson blotch in throat. Many blooms open. This is very pretty and liked by everyone. I am confident it will be a best seller when known.

LA PALOMA. (DUSINBERRE) Very bright vivid orange. A new shade different from any other. Large flowers (4-5 inches across) 4-6 open. Texture like leather. Tall, strong healthy grower. Bulblets grow stronger than any other variety on my place.

12

This has the livest and most vivid orange color of any large flowered orange I have seen. It does not fade, burn or streak.

Carl Salbach, E. F. Palmer, J. H. Heberling and other famous growers say it was very fine with them the past season and they like it very much. Growers who saw it at Springfield told me they thought it had the brightest future of any new glad on the market. You had better try it.

LAUGHING WATERS. (STEPHEN) Beautiful pink, many open. Well liked by garden visitors.

LAURETTA. (KEMP) Seedling of Golden Measure. Orange pink with yellow throat. Petals tipped dark red.

LAVENDER ROSE. (K) Very beautiful new shade of lavender rose. Soft yellow blotch. A nice thing.

LEWIS DINGMAN. (GOODRICH) A beautiful smoky with red blotch. This has a velvety appearance seen in no other smoky. Really fine.

LILAC GLORY. (K) Large soft lilac rose pink, darker throat. Several open.

LILAC WONDER. (GRULLEMANS) Very early, tall clear lilac lavender.

LILY OF GOLD. (K) Clear, rich canary yellow, little darker on lower petals. Heavily ruffled and a new type of flower. Upper petals much larger than lower ones. Short grower.

LLEWELLYN. (SALBACH) Heavily ruffled seedling of Pink Lily. Taller, little lighter with cream throat. Very popular.

LONDON SMOKE. (D) Dark smoky pink overlaid with slate. One of the best smokies and almost exactly like a new variety put out last year at a high price.

LONGFELLOW. (DECORAH) Large wide open La France pink. Several perfectly placed blooms open. A coming commercial.

LORICE. (KEMP) Salmon orange overlaid with scarlet, cream lip. Several open. Tall, strong grower. This does not seem to be well known but nearly everyone who has tried it likes it very much. Have had many orders from those to whom I sent trial bulbs.

LOS ANGELES. (HOUDYSHELL) Delicate pink with cerise feather in the throat. Called the cut and come again gladiolus as it often sends out spikes after the main one has been cut. A good variety.

LOUVAIN. (GROPP) Medium light pink sometimes flaked darker. Several perfectly placed blooms open. Large flowers with texture like leather. A fine thing. Should make a good commercial. In fact some consider it the best commercial type pink on the market.

LOYALTY. (AUSTIN) Perfectly clear yellow about the shade of Golden Dream. Large flowers, many open at a time. Very tall. Strong grower with immense foilage. Many consider this the finest yellow on the market. Wonderful for exhibition. It won at Springfield in competition with good Golden Dream and Tobersun. It won a silver cup at Boston. A. L. Stephen the famous exhibitor says it is the finest yellow. Mrs. Austin introduced this but last year I bought her entire stock which is very limited as yet. Good propagator.

MME. MOUNET SULLY. (LEMOINE) Cream white with bright red blotch bordered pale yellow. Several open. Very striking. Always in demand.

MAMMOTH WHITE. (UNITED BULB) Immense pure white, 6 inches or more across, 5-6 open. Great exhibition variety.

MARIETTA. (METZNER) Very large light salmon tinged with orange. Shading into a flame red blotch. Very pretty.

MARIE KUNDERD. (K) The finest early white glad. Beautiful ruffled snow white with faint pink lines in the throat. Good substance A very fine thing.

MARMORA. (ERREY) Sport of Emile Auburn. The same in habit and growth and propagating qualities but a wonderful gray color with pale purplish blotch. 8-10 or more perfectly placed blooms open at a time. Wonderful for exhibition and will be grown by the million for cut flowers. The florists will scramble for this one as it is extremely beautiful and there is nothing else like it. Very fine when used with a good clear yellow like Golden Dream. Too much cannot be said for this variety.

13

Marmora

Mother Machree

Marnia

14

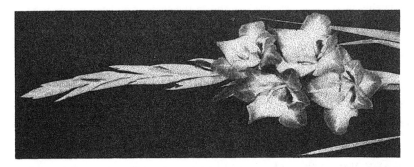

J. T. Pirie

Pfitzer's Triumph

Mrs. P. W. Sisson

Minuet

I probably have the largest stock of this in the country and can supply most any quantity.

MARNIA. (KEMP) A beautiful live orange slightly tinged pink, practically an orange self, 4-6 large blooms open. Tall, strong grower. Great commercial variety. The best large flowered commercial orange on the market. You better try it.

MARSHALL FOCH. (K) Beautiful large light salmon pink with darker spot in the throat. Fine commercial.

MARY FREY. (GELSER) Lavender pink somewhat similar in color to Mrs. Peters but a softer, warmer shade and a month earlier. Several open. Has a willowy stem very suitable for florist use. Its earliness also makes it valuable as a florist flower. This has been fine the past season.

MARY JANE. (K) Light, silvery lavender. Several open.

MILADY IMOGENE. (AUSTIN) Medium sized pure ruffled white on a tall willowy spike. Many open. This looks like a very fine florist white. Haven't seen any better.

MILLIONAIRE. (K) Very nice velvety red, creamy blotches in throat.

MINUET. (COLEMAN) The lavender by which all other lavenders are judged. Wonderfully beautiful clear light lavender. 4-6 very large heavily textured blooms open. This variety has character stamped all over it. Heavy strong foilage. To my mind there is no better lavender in existence.

MISS DES MOINES. (DECORAH) Beautiful clear lavender shading to creamy white throat. Many blooms open at a time. Won the Sisson prize at the Des Moines Show for best seedling in the show. I have not bloomed this my self but understand it is very fine.

MISS TEA ROSE. (FISCHER) Creamy tea rose color. Large blooms. Distinctive.

MISS UNIVERSE. (K) Bright tyrian red with darker blotch.

MOROCCO. (PF.) Very deep red almost black. Large fine. The best in this color.

MOTHER MACHREE. (STEVENS) Vinaceous lavender overlaid toward the edges of petals with a sort of salmon pink. The color is difficult to describe but it is very beautiful. When opened in the house it has a translucent appearance which greatly increases its beauty. Might be called a smoky but not really one and much better than any smoky.

Tall, straight plant with 6-10 large well placed blooms open. The habit and growth of Mother Machree I would call nearly ideal. The color some people don't like but most people rave over. I was one of the introducers of this variety so may be prejudiced but those who ought to know tell me that it will be in big demand by the better class of florists when stock is available.

J. W. Crow the well known grower of Simcoe, Ontario, wrote me last year, "It's all true. Mother Machree was shown at the Canadian Show at Lindsay and was the sensation of the show. The color is exquisite and the shading wonderful. For such a massive flower and spike the form of both was most striking and of special interest to me who worship gracefulness. If this informality is characteristic the variety is due for immense popularity. I have seen nothing to compare with it."

MR. MARK. (VELTHUYS) Tall dark blue. The best at the price.

MRS. ANNA PFITZER. (PF.) Tall creamy white with long spike of well placed flowers. Buds greenish. One of Pfitzer's finest varieties.

MRS. CATHERINE EDWARDS. (HORNBERGER) Large cream white, long spike with many blooms open.

MRS. CHAS. A. STEVENS. (K) Mallow purple flaked deeper. Several open.

MRS. ELLA MORRISON. (KIRCHHOPE) Very tall growing light pink sometimes flaked deeper pink. Very large flowers. A fine variety either for the garden or as a commercial.

January, 1930

GLADIOLUS PRICE LIST

Champlain View Gardens

ELMER E. GOVE

BURLINGTON, VERMONT

At these prices all bulbs are prepaid anywhere in the United States and Canada and all countries in the Postal Union.

The PACKAGES of Bulblets contain from twenty to one hundred or more bulblets, according to variety. The cheaper varieties contain more than the others. They are not counted but all are big value.

5 at 10 rate, 25 at 100 rate; Bulblets, 250 at 1000 rate.

On cash orders of $50, I will give 1 No. 6 Mother Machree free. On $100 orders I will give 1 No. 1 Mother Machree. In addition to this on a $25 cash order you can select 5% extra bulbs. On a $50 order add 10% of bulbs. On a $100 order add 20% of bulbs. It will pay you to get your friends and neighbors to pool their orders with you. These offers are for cash with order, and orders must contain at least 3 varieties to get the discount.

	Per	No. 1	No. 2	No. 3	No. 4	No. 5	No. 6	BULBLETS Per	
A. B. Kunderd.......	1	.10	.08	.07	....	....	....	Pkg.	.10
	10	.60	.50	.40	.30	.20	.10	1000	.75
	100	4.00	3.00	2.40	1.75	1.20	.80	Qt.	2.50
	1000	35.00	30.00	25.00	18.00	10.00	6.00		
A. E. Kunderd.......	1	.60	.50	.40	.30	.20	.15	Pkg.	.25
	10	4.80	4.00	3.20	2.40	1.60	1.20	1000	20.00
Albatross...........		Sold out						....	....
Al. Smith...........	1	....	....	.60	.40	.30	.20	1	.10
Ambrosia...........	1	6.00	5.00	4.00	3.00	2.00	1.00	1	.50
Amethyst..........	1	1.00	.80	.60	....	....	....	1	.10
Angel's Dream.......	1	6.00	5.00	4.00	3.00	2.00	1.00	1	.60
Anna Eberius........	1	.10	.08	.07	....	....	....	Pkg.	.10
	10	.60	.50	.40	.30	.20	.10	1000	1.00
Annie Laurie........	1	.20	.15	.10	....	....	....	Pkg.	.20
	10	1.50	1.25	1.00	.75	.50	.35	1000	3.00
	100	10.00	8.00	5.00	3.50	2.50	1.50	Qt.	10.00
	1000	90.00	70.00	40.00	28.00	20.00	12.00	Pk.	50.00
Anthony Zonker.....	1	.15	.12	.10	....	....	....	Pkg.	.15
	10	1.20	.90	.75	.50	.40	.25	1000	1.00
	100	....	5.00	4.00	3.00	2.00	1.25	....	....
Antione............	1	1.50	1.25	1.00	.75	.50	.30	10	1.00
	10	....	....	8.00	6.00	4.00	2.00	100	6.00
Antonia Antonette...	1	.25	.20	.15	.10	....	....	Pkg.	.25
	10	2.00	1.60	1.20	.80	.60	.40	1000	1.00
	100	12.00	10.00	8.00	6.00	4.00	2.50	Qt.	3.00

	Per	No. 1	No. 2	No. 3	No. 4	No. 5	No. 6	Bulblets Per	
Ave Maria	1	5.00	4.50	4.00	3.00	2.00	----	1	.40
Bengal Tiger	1	.10	.08	.07	----	----	----	Pa.	.10
	10	.80	.65	.50	.35	----	----	1000	1.00
	100	4.00	3.20	2.65	2.00	----	----		
Berty Snow	1	1.00	.80	.60	----	----	----	10	1.00
Betty Nuthall	1	4.00	3.00	2.00	1.50	1.00	.75	15	1.00
	10	20.00	17.50	15.00	8.00	7.00	5.00	100	5.00
	100	100.00	90.00	80.00	70.00	50.00	30.00	1000	27.00
Blanche Bollinger	1	.15	.12	.10	----	----	----	Pkg.	.15
	10	1.20	.90	.75	.60	.45	.30	1000	1.00
	100	6.00	5.00	4.00	3.00	2.20	1.40	Qt.	2.00
Bleeding Heart	1	1.00	.85	.75	----	.55	.45	5	.25
	10	8.00	6.50	5.00	----	3.00	2.00	100	4.00
Blue Torch	1	.15	.12	.10	----	----	----	Pkg.	.15
	10	1.20	.95	.80	.65	.45	.30	1000	1.00
	100	8.00	6.00	5.00	4.00	3.00	2.00	Qt.	3.00
	1000	55.00	45.00	37.50	30.00	24.00	16.00	Pk.	15.00
Blushes of Cream	1	----	1.25	1.00	.75	.50	.35	1	.15
Bobby	1	.20	.15	.10	----	----	----	Pkg.	.20
	10	1.00	.85	.70	----	.40	.25	1000	2.00
	100	9.00	8.00	6.00	----	3.00	2.00	Qt.	5.00
Break O'Day	1	.10	.08	.07	----	----	----	Pkg.	.10
	10	.80	.65	.50	.40	.30	.20	1000	1.00
Bridal Veil	1	1.00	.80	.60	.40	.30	.20	10	.50
Byron L. Smith	1	----	.10	.07	----	----	----	Pkg.	.10
	10	----	.60	.50	----	----	----	1000	1.00
	100	5.00	4.00	3.20	----	----	----	Qt.	2.00
Cabernet	1	1.00	.80	.60	.45	.35	.25	10	.50
California	1	1.25	1.00	.75	.50	.35	.25	10	.75
	10	10.00	8.00	6.00	4.00	2.50	1.50	100	5.00
Canberra	1	2.50	2.00	1.50	----	----	----	1	.25
	10	20.00	16.00	----	----	----	----		.10
Capt. Boynton	1	.10	.08	.07	----	----	----	Pkg.	.10
	10	.80	.70	.60	.50	.40	.30	1000	1.00
	100	5.00	4.00	3.00	2.20	1.40	.75	Qt.	3.50
	1000	40.00	32.00	24.00	18.00	12.00	6.00		
Cardinal Prince	1	.15	.12	.10	----	----	----	Pkg.	.25
	10	1.20	.90	.70	.50	.35	.20	1000	1.00
	100	8.00	6.40	3.00	2.00	1.50	1.00	Qt.	3.50
	1000	60.00	45.00	35.00	25.00	15.00	8.00	Pk.	20.00
Carolus Clusius	1	1.00	.80	.60	.45	.35	.25	5	.25
	10	7.00	6.00	4.00	3.00	2.00	1.00	1000	25.00
	100	50.00	40.00	30.00	20.00	15.00	10.00	Qt.	50.00
	1000	----	----	----	150.00	120.00	80.00	----	----
Catherine Coleman	1	.25	.20	.15	.12	.10	----	Pkg.	.25
	10	2.00	1.60	1.20	----	.80	.60	1000	5.00
	100	15.00	12.00	10.00	----	6.00	4.00		
Cattleya Rose	1	1.00	.80	.60	.40	.30	.20	5	.25
Chas. F. Fairbanks	1	.10	.08	.07	----	----	----	Pkg.	.10
	10	.80	.65	.50	----	----	----	1000	1.00
Cherry Rose	1	.30	.25	.20	.15	.10	----	Pkg.	.25
	10	2.40	2.00	1.60	1.20	.80	.50	1000	3.00
Chicago	1	2.00	1.50	1.00	.75	.50	----	1	.25
Color Marvel	1	2.50	2.00	1.50	1.00	.75	.50	1	.25
Coronado	1	5.00	3.50	2.50	1.50	1.00	----	3	1.00
Coryphee	1	2.50	2.00	1.50	1.25	1.00	.75	10	1.00
	10	20.00	16.00	12.00	10.00	8.50	6.00	100	9.00
	100	160.00	125.00	100.00	75.00	60.00	40.00	1000	80.00

	Per	No. 1	No. 2	No. 3	No. 4	No. 5	No. 6	BULBLETS Per	
Crimson Glow.......	1	.10	.08	.07	....	....	....	Pkg.	.10
	10	.70	.60	.50	40	.30	.20	1000	.75
	100	....	3.25	2.50	1.50	1.00	.75	Qt.	1.25
	1000	....	....	17.00	14.00	8.00	5.00	....	....
Crinkles............	1	.15	.12	.10	....	....	....	Pkg.	.15
	10	1.20	.90	.70	.50	.35	.25	1000	1.50
Desdemone.........	1	.25	.20	.15	.10	....	....	Pkg.	.25
	10	2.00	1.60	1.20	....	.60	.40	1000	2.50
	100	15.00	12.00	10.00	....	5.00	3.00	....	....
Dominus...........	1	....	....	2.00	1.50	1.00	.75	1	.25
Dorcas Aldrich.......	1	.60	.50	.40	.30	.20	.10	10	.35
	10	5.00	4.00	3.00	2.00	1.25	.75	1000	10.00
Dorritt.............	1	.10	.08	.07	....	....	....	Pkg.	.10
	10	.70	.60	.50	40	.30	.20	1000	1.00
	100	5.00	4.00	3.00	2.00	1.00	.65	Qt.	3.00
Dr. Christ Martz.....	1	.20	.15	.10	....	....	....	Pkg.	.20
	10	1.60	1.20	.80	.60	.50	.40	1000	2.00
	100	10.00	8.00	6.00	5.00	4.00	3.00	Qt.	5.00
Dr. F. E. Bennett....	1	.15	.12	.10	....	....	....	Pkg.	.15
	10	1.20	.95	.80	.70	.60	.50	1000	2.50
	100	8.00	6.40	3.50	2.75	1.75	1.25	Qt.	7.50
Dr. L. H. Bailey.....	1	3.00	2.50	2.00	1.50	1.00	....	1	.25
Dr. Moody..........	1	1.25	1.00	.75	.60	.50	.40	5	.50
	10	11.00	9.00	7.00	5.50	4.00	3.00	100	4.00
	100	75.00	50.00	25.00	20.00	15.00	10.00	1000	20.00
Dr. Nelson Shook....	1	.50	.40	.30	.25	.20	.15	10	.25
	10	4.00	3.20	2.40	2.00	1.60	1.20	100	2.00
	100	30.00	25.00	20.00	16.00	12.00	10.00	1000	15.00
Dr. Starkweather.....	1	....	....	1.00	.75	.50	.35	1	.15
Dr. W. Van Fleet....	1	.10	.08	.07	....	....	....	Pkg.	.10
	10	.50	.45	.40	....	....	....	1000	.75
	100	3.50	3.00	2.50	....	....	....	Qt.,	1.50
Duchess of York.....	1	.15	.12	.10	....	....	....	Pkg.	.15
	10	1.00	.80	.60	.40	.30	.20	1000	1.50
	100	8.00	6.00	4.50	3.00	2.00	1.25		
Early Phipps........	1	4.00	3.50	2.50	2.00	1.50	1.00	Each	.50
Ed. Springer........	1	.25	.20	.15	.10	....	....	Pkg.	.25
E. G. Hill..........	1	.10	.08	.07	....	....	....	Pkg.	.10
	10	.70	.60	.50	.40	.30	.20	1000	.75
	100	4.00	3.50	3.00	2.00	....	....	Qt.	2.00
Eighth Wonder......	1	.75	.65	.55	.45	.35	.25	1	.10
	10	6.00	5.00	4.00	3.00	2.00	1.25	100	5.00
Elf................	1	.10	.08	.07	....	....	....	Pkg.	.10
	10	.65	.55	.45	....	....	....	1000	.75
	100	4.00	3.00	2.00	....	....	....	Qt.	1.50
Ella Day...........	1	2.50	2.00	1.50	1.00	.75	.50	1	.25
Elrose.............	1	1.50	1.25	1.00	.75	.50	.35	1	.15
Emile Auburn.......	1	.25	.20	.15	.10	....	....	Pkg.	.25
	10	2.00	1.60	1.20	.80	.60	.50	1000	2.50
	100	15.00	12.00	10.00	8.00	5.00	3.00	Qt.	10.00
	1000	100.00	80.00	60.00	40.00	30.00	20.00	Pk.	50.00
Ensign.............	1	.75	.60	.50	.40	30.	.20	10	.50
Eugene Lefebvre.....	1	.20	.15	.10	....	....	....	Pkg.	.20
	10	1.60	1.20	.80	.60	.40	.25	Pkg.	.20
Excellence..........	1	.20	.15	.10	....	....	....	Pkg.	.15
	10	1.50	1.25	1.00	.75	.50	.25	1000	1.50
Faith..............	1	15.00	12.00	....	....	....	....	1	2.00
Fay Lamphier.......	1	.10	.08	.07	....	....	....	Pkg.	.10
	10	.80	.70	.60	.50	.40	.30	1000	2.00
	100	5.00	4.00	3.00	2.50	2.00	1.00	Qt.	4.00

	Per	No. 1	No. 2	No. 3	No. 4	No. 5	No. 6	BULBLETS Per	
Fern Kyle..........	1	.10	.08	.07	....	....	....	Pkg.	.10
	10	.70	.60	.50	.40	.30	.20	1000	1.00
	100	4.00	3.50	3.00	2.00	1.50	1.00	Qt.	2.00
	1000	35.00	30.00	25.00	18.00	12.00	8.00	Pk.	10.00
Fire Glow..........	1	....	....	.60	.40	.30	.25	1	.10
Fire Pink...........	1	....	....	1.00	.75	.50	.35	1	.15
Fontaine...........	1	.10	.08	.07	....	....	....	Pkg.	.10
	10	.70	.60	.50	.40	.30	.20	1000	1.00
	100	4.00	3.00	2.40	1.80	1.20	.80	Qt.	2.00
	1000	35.00	25.00	20.00	16.00	10.00	6.00	Pk.	10.00
Frank J. Symmes....	1	.10	.08	.07	....	....	....	Pkg.	.10
	10	.70	.60	.50	....	....	....	1000	1.00
	100	4.00	3.50	3.00	....	....	....	Qt.	2.00
	1000	35.00	30.00	25.00	....	....	....		
Fuld's Favorite......	1	.50	.40	.30	.25	.20	.15	5	.25
Gay Hussar.........	1	1.50	1.00	.75	.50	.35	.20	10	.50
	10	7.50	7.00	6.00	4.00	3.00	1.50	100	2.00
	100	60.00	55.00	40.00	30.00	20.00	12.50	1000	15.00
Gene Stratton Porter.	1	....	.15	.10	....	....	....	Pkg.	.15
	10	....	....	.70	.50	.35	.25	....	....
Georgeous..........	1	....	....	1.00	.75	.50	.35	1	.15
Geraldine Farrar.....	1	.30	.25	.20	.15	.10	.50	Pkg.	.25
	10	2.40	2.00	1.60	1.20	.80	....	....	....
Gertrude Errey......	1	.15	.12	.10	....	....	....	Pkg.	.15
	10	1.20	.95	.80	.65	.45	.25	1000	1.00
	100	8.00	6.00	4.00	3.00	2.00	1.25	Qt.	3.00
Gertrude Pfitzer......	1	2.50	2.00	1.50	1.00	.75	.50	1	.25
	10	20.00	16.00	12.00	8.00	6.00	4.00	100	20.00
Giant Nymph........	1	.10	.08	.07	....	....	....	Pkg.	.10
	10	.60	.50	.40	.30	.20	.10	1000	.75
	100	4.00	3.00	2.40	....	....	....	Qt.	1.50
	1000	35.00	30.00	25.00	....	....	....	Pk.	8.00
Gloriana...........	1	.30	.25	.20	.15	.10	....	Pkg.	.25
	10	2.40	2.00	1.60	1.20	.80	.50	1000	4.00
	100	15.00	12.00	....	....	4.00	2.50	Qt.	14.00
	1000	120.00	90.00	....	....	....	18.00	Pk.	75.00
Glory of U. S. A.....	1	10.00	10.00	7.00	7.00	5.00	....	1	.25
Gold..............	1	.10	08	.07	....	....	....	Pkg.	.10
	10	....	.50	.40	....	....	....	1000	.80
	100	....	3.50	2.50	....	....	....	....	....
Gold Eagle.........	1	.20	.15	.10	....	....	....	Pkg.	.20
	10	1.60	1.20	.95	.60	.50	.40	1000	2.50
	100	12.00	9.00	6.00	4.75	3.00	....	....	....
	1000	80.00	65.00	50.00	40.00	25.00	....	....	....
Golden Brown.......	1	....	1.25	1.00	.75	.50	.35	1	.15
Golden Dream........	1	.40	.35	.30	.25	.20	.15	10	.25
	10	3.20	2.75	2.25	1.75	1.25	.75	1000	8.00
	100	18.00	15.00	12.00	10.00	8.00	5.00	Qt.	25.00
	1000	150.00	120.00	90.00	75.00	60.00	40.00	Pk.	150.00
Golden Measure......	1	.10	.08	.07	....	....	....	Pkg.	.10
	10	.65	.55	.45	.35	.25	.15	1000	1.00
	100	4.00	3.00	2.50	2.00	1.50	.75	Qt.	3.00
Golden Salmon.......	1	.25	.20	.15	.10	....	....	Pkg.	.25
	10	2.00	1.60	1.20	.80	.60	.40	1000	2.00
	100	15.00	12.00	9.00	7.00	5.00	3.00	....	....
Golden Snapdragon...	1	.50	.40	.30	.20	.10	....	10	.50
	10	4.00	3.20	2.40	1.60	.80	....	100	2.00
Grace Kimball.......	1	.50	.40	.30	....	....	....	....	....
Grand Guardian.....	1	7.00	6.00	5.00	4.00	3.00	2.00·	1	.50

	Per	No. 1	No. 2	No. 3	No. 4	No. 5	No. 6	BULBLETS Per	
Hamburg Pink......	1	1.50	1.00	.75	....	....	....	1	.15
Heavenly Blue......	1	1.00	.80	.60	.50	.40	.30	Pkg.	.50
	10	9.00	8.00	7.00	6.00	5.00	4.00	100	4.00
	100	....	....	....	....	40.00	30.00	1000	30.00
H. Kanzleiter........	1	.10	.08	.07	....	....	....	Pkg.	.10
	10	.70	.60	.50	.40	.30	.20	1000	1.00
	100	4.00	3.50	2.25	1.50	1.00	.60	Qt.	2.50
Helen Howard......	1	.45	.40	.30	.20	.10	....	Pkg.	.25
	10	4.00	3.20	2.40	1.60	.80	.50	100	.75
	100	25.00	15.00	10.00	7.00	5.00	3.00	1000	5.00
Helen Phipps........	1	1.50	1.25	1.00	.75	.60	.40	1	.15
	10	10.00	9.00	8.00	6.00	4.50	3.00	10	.75
	100	75.00	65.00	55.00	45.00	35.00	25.00	100	2.50
Helen Wills	1	.75	.65	.50	.40	.30	.20	10	.25
	10	4.00	3.00	2.50	1.75	1.25	1.00	100	1.00
	100	30.00	25.00	20.00	15.00	10.00	8.00	1000	5.00
H. C. Goehl........	1	.15	.12	.10	....	....	....	Pkg.	.15
	10	.90	.80	.70	.60	.50	.40	1000	1.00
	100	5.00	4.00	3.00	2.20	1.40	1.00	....	....
Herbert Hoover......	1	....	....	.60	.40	.30	.20	1	.10
Herbstzauber........	1	.35	.30	.25	.20	.15	.10	Pkg.	.25
	10	2.00	1.75	1.50	1.20	1.00	.75	100	.70
	100	16.00	14.00	12.00	10.00	6.00	4.00	1000	6.00
	1000	....	90.00	70.00	50.00	35.00	20.00	Qt.	20.00
Highland Laddie.....	1	.15	.12	.10	....	....	....	Pkg.	.15
	10	.80	.70	.60	.50	.40	.30	1000	1.00
High Nye..........	1	.15	.12	.10	....	....	....	Pkg.	.10
	10	1.20	.90	.80	.70	.60	.50	100	.50
	100	8.00	6.00	5.00	4.00	3.00	2.00	1000	3.00
	1000	70.00	60.00	48.00	32.00	24.00	16.00	Qt.	5.00
Impressario..........	1	....	7.50	5.00	....	....	....	1	.75
Indian Chief.........	1	.50	.40	.30	.20	.10	....	Pkg.	.25
Indian Summer......	1	.20	.15	.10	....	....	....	Pkg	.20
	10	1.60	1.20	.80	.60	.50	.40	100	.60
Inspiration..........		All Sizes $10.00							
Iver'l..............	1	3.00	2.50	....	....	....	....	1	.40
Iwa...............	1	.15	.10	.07	....	....	....	Pkg.	.15
	10	1.20	.80	.50	.40	.30	.20	1000	1.50
	100	8.00	6.00	4.00	....	2.00	1.00	Qt.	4.00
	1000	60.00	50.00	35.00	....	12.00	7.50	Pk.	25.00
Jacelia..............	1	....	....	.60	.40	.30	.20	1	.10
J. V. Beijeren........	1	.10	.08	.07	....	....	....	Pkg.	.10
	10	.75	.65	.55	....	....	....	1000	1.00
	100	....	4.00	3.00	....	....	....	....	....
Jane Addams........	1	.50	.40	.30	.25	.20	.15	10	.25
Jap Lady...........	1	.20	.15	.10	....	....	....	10	.25
	10	....	1.20	.80	.60	.40	.25	....	....
Jean Du Taillis......	1	.20	.15	.10	....	....	....	Pkg.	.20
	10	1.60	1.20	.80	....	....	....	....	....
Jenny Lind..........	1	.10	.08	.07	....	....	....	Pkg.	.10
	10	.70	.60	.50	.40	.30	.20	1000	1.00
	100	5.00	4.00	3.00	2.20	1.40	1.00	Qt.	3.50
	1000	....	36.00	27.00	20.00	12.50	8.00	Pk.	20.00
J. H. McFarland.....	1	2.00	1.50	1.00	.75	.50	....	1	.25
Joerg's White........	1	.50	.40	.30	.20	.15	.10	Pkg.	.30
	10	4.00	3.20	2.40	1.60	1.20	.80	100	1.70
J. O. Armour........	1	.15	.10	.07	....	....	....	Pkg.	.15
	10	1.00	.80	.60	.40	.30	.20	1000	1.00
	100	8.00	6.00	4.50	3.00	2.00	1.25	Qt.	3.00

	Per	No. 1	No. 2	No. 3	No. 4	No. 5	No. 6	BULBLETS Per	
Jonkheer Van Tets...	1	5.00	4.50	4.00	....	....	....	1	.50
J. T. McCutcheon....	1	.20	.15	.10	....	....	....	Pkg.	.25
	10	1.60	1.20	.80	.60	.40	.25	1000	1.50
	100	10 00	8.00	6.00	4.50	3.00	1.50	Qt.	4.00
J. T. Pirie..........	1	.10	.08	.07	....	....	....	Pkg.	.10
	10	.80	.65	.50	.40	.30	.20	1000	1.00
	100	6.50	5.50	4.50	3.50	2.50	1.50	Qt.	4.00
King George........	1	1.25	1.00	.75	....	....	....	1	.20
King of Reds.......	1	....	....	....	.75	.50	.35	1	.15
King Tut...........	1	2.50	2.00	....	....	....	....	1	.25
Kirchhoff's Apple	1	.20	.15	.10	....	....	....	Pkg.	.20
Blossom..........	10	1.60	1.20	.80	....	.45	.30	1000	1.50
Rirchhoff's Violet....	1	.25	.20	.15	....	....	....	....	....
	10	2.00	1.75	1.40	....	....	....	....	....
	100	18.00	15.00	12.00	....	....	....	....	....
Kund's Apple Blossom	1	.10	.08	.07	....	....	....	Pkg.	.10
	10	.70	.60	.50	....	....	....	1000	1.00
	100	5.00	4.00	3.00	....	....	....	Qt.	2.00
Kund's Yellow	1	.25	.20	.15	.10	....	....	Pkg.	.25
Favorite..........	10	2.00	1.60	1.20	.80	.50	.30	1000	2.00
	100	10.00	8.00	6.00	5.00	3.00	2.00	....	....
Kund's Yellow Won...	1	.30	.25	.20	.15	.10	....	Pkg.	.25
Wonder..........	10	2.40	2.00	1.60	1.20	.80	.60	1000	1.00
	100	12.00	8.00	4.50	3.50	2.00	1.25	Qt.	3.50
	1000	....	65.00	35.00	20.00	15.00	10.00	....	....
Lacinatus..........	1	.10	.08	.07	....	....	....	Pkg.	.10
	10	.60	.50	.40	.30	.20	.10	1000	1.00
	100	....	4.00	3.00	2.00	1.25	.80	Qt.	2.00
Laidley............	1	1.00	.75	....	....	....	....	....	....
La Paloma.........	1	5.00	4.00	3.00	2.00	1.25	1.00	No bbts.	
	10	40.00	32.00	24.00	16.00	10.00	8.00	....	....
	100	300.00	250.00	175.00	125.00	80.00	50.00	....	....
Laughing Waters.....	1	.50	.40	.30	.20	.15	.10	10	.40
	10	4.00	3.20	2.40	1.60	1.20	.80	1000	30.00
	100	30.00	25.00	20.00	15.00	10.00	....	....	....
Lauretta..........	1	.25	.20	.15	.10	....	....	Pkg.	.25
	10	2.00	1.60	1.20	.80	.60	.40	1000	1.50
Lavender Rose.......	1	6.00	5.00	4.00	3.00	2.00	1.00	1	.50
Lewis Dingman...,...	1	.15	.12	10	....	....	....	Pkg.	.25
	10	1.20	.90	.70	.50	.35	.25	1000	1.50
Lilac Glory	1	.10	.08	.07	....	....	....	Pkg.	.10
	10	.70	.60	.50	....	•......	....	1000	1.00
	100	....	5.00	4.00	....	....	....	....	....
Lilac Wonder........	1	.15	.12	.10	....	....	....	Pkg.	.15
	10	1.20	.90	.70	.50	.35	.70	1000	1.50
	100	10.00	8.00	6.00	4.00	2.00	1.25	Qt.	3.00
Lily of Gold........	1	25.00	20.00	15.00	12.50	10.00	7.50	1	1.50
Llewellyn..........	1	.15	.10	....	....	....	....	Pkg.	.15
	10	1.20	.90	.60	.40	.30	.20	1000	2.00
	100	10.00	8.00	5.00	3.00	2.00	1.50	....	....
London Smoke.......	1	.15	.12	.10	....	....	....	Pkg.	.15
	10	1.00	.80	.60	.40	.25	.15	1000	1.00
	100	5.00	4.00	3.00	2.20	1.40	1.00	Qt.	3.50
Longfellow..........	1	.20	.15	.10	....	....	....	Pkg.	.20
	10	1.60	1.25	.75	.60	.40	.25	1000	2.50
	100	10.00	8.00	5.00	3.50	2.40	1.25	Qt.	9.00

6

	Per	No. 1	No. 2	No. 3	No. 4	No. 5	No. 6	BULBLETS Per	
Lorice	1	.20	.15	.10	....	....	....	Pkg.	.20
	10	1.60	1.20	.80	.60	.45	.30	1000	1.50
	100	10.00	8.00	6.00	....	3.00	2.00	Qt.	4.00
	1000	80.00	60.00	45.00	....	20.00	15.00	Pk.	20.00
Los Angeles	1	.10	.08	.07	....	....	....	Pkg.	.10
	10	.60	.50	.40	.30	.20	.10	1000	.75
	100	5.00	4.00	2.25	1.50	1.00	.60	Qt.	1.50
Louvain	1	.25	.20	.15	.10	....	....	Pkg.	.25
	10	2.00	1.60	1.20	.80	.60	.40	1000	2.00
Loyalty	1	1.50	1.25	1.00	.75	.50	.25	5	.50
	10	12.00	10.00	8.00	6.00	4.00	....	100	7.00
	100	90.00	70.00	60.00	40.00	30.00	....	1000	50.00
M. M. Sully	1	.30	.25	.20	....	....	....	....	....
	10	2.40	2.00	1.60	....	....	....	....	....
Mammoth White	1	6.00	5.00	4.00	3.00	2.00	1.00	1	.50
	10	....	....	30.00	20.00	15.00	8.00	10	4.00
Marietta	1	.10	.08	.07	....	....	....	Pkg.	.10
	10	.80	.70	.60	.50	.40	.30	1000	2.00
	100	....	5.00	4.00	3.00	2.00	1.00	....	....
Marie Kunderd	10	....	....	....	.30	.20	.15	Pkg.	.25
	100	....	....	....	2.00	1.25	.75	1000	1.50
Marmora	1	1.00	.80	.60	.40	.30	.20	10	.45
	10	8.00	6.00	4.50	3.00	2.50	2.00	100	1.50
	100	50.00	40.00	30.00	25.00	20.00	15.00	1000	10.00
	1000	400.00	320.00	240.00	200.00	160.00	120.00	Qt.	40.00
Marnia	1	.15	.12	.10	....	....	....	Pkg.	.15
	10	1.00	.80	.60	.45	.30	.20	1000	2.00
	100	6.00	5.00	4.00	3.00	2.00	1.00	Qt.	5.00
	1000	50.00	40.00	30.00	20.00	12.00	7.50	Pk.	25.00
Mar. Foch	1	.10	.08	.07	....	....	....	Pkg.	.10
	10	.65	.55	.45	....	....	....	1000	.80
	100	4.00	3.00	2.40	....	....	....	Qt.	3.00
	1000	....	30.00	25.00	....	....	....	Pk.	16.00
Mary Frey	1	1.25	1.00	.80	.60	.50	.40	5	.40
	10	10.00	8.00	6.40	4.80	4.00	3.20	100	4.00
	100	40.00	30.00	20.00	15.00	12.00	8.00	1000	10.00
	1000	....	....	150.00	120.00	90.00	65.00	Qt.	45.00
Mary Jane	1	.50	.40	.30	....	....	....	Pkg.	.25
	10	4.00	3.20	2.40	....	....	....	100	2.00
Milady Imogene	1	.50	.40	.35	.25	.20	.15	10	.50
Millionaire	1	.20	.15	.10	....	....	....	Pkg.	.20
	10	....	1.20	.80	.60	.40	.20	1000	2.00
Minuet	1	.75	.60	.50	.40	.30	.20	Pkg.	.35
	10	6.00	5.00	4.00	3.00	2.00	1.00	1000	20.00
	100	40.00	30.00	....	....	....	....	....	....
Miss Des Moines	1	10.00	7.50	4.00	3.00	2.00	1.25	1	.35
Miss Tea Rose	1	.15	.12	.10	....	....	....	Pkg.	.15
	10	1.00	.80	.60	.50	.35	.20	1000	1.50
	100	....	6.00	5.00	3.50	2.00	1.25	Qt.	3.00
Miss Universe	1	....	....	4.00	3.00	2.00	1.00	1	.50
Morocco	1	5.00	4.00	3.50	3.00	2.50	....	1	.50
Mother Machree	1	25.00	20.00	15.00	10.00	7.50	5.00	1	1.00
	10	200.00	160.00	120.00	80.00	60.00	40.00	10	8.00
Mr. Mark	1	.10	.08	.07	....	....	....	Pkg.	.10
	10	.70	.60	.50	....	....	....	1000	2.00
	100	....	4.00	3.00	2.00	....	....	....	....
Mrs. Anna Pfitzer	1	4.00	3.50	3.00	....	....	....	....	....
Mrs. C. Edwards	1	50.00	40.00	30.00	20.00	15.00	10.00	1	2.50
Mrs. Chas. A. Stevens	1	....	....	1.00	.75	.50	.35	1	.15

	Per	No. 1	No. 2	No. 3	No. 4	No. 5	No. 6	BULBLETS Per	
Mrs. Ella Morrison...	1	.20	.15	.10	....	....	....	Pkg.	.20
	10	1.60	1.20	.80	.50	.35	.25	1000	.75
	100	7.00	5.00	3.00	·2.00	1.00	.75	Qt.	2.00
	1000	....	....	25.00	18.00	12.00	6.00	....	....
Mrs. F. C. Hornberger	1	.35	.30	.25	.20	.15	.10	Pkg.	.25
	10	2.50	2.00	1.50	1.25	1.00	.75	100	.75
	100	16.00	12.00	8.00	6.00	4.00	2.00	1000	2.00
	1000	....	90.00	60.00	50.00	35.00	20.00	Qt.	8.00
Mrs. F. C. Peters....	1	.10	.08	.07	....	....	....	Pkg.	.10
	10	.60	.50	.40	.30	.20	.10	1000	.75
	100	4.00	3.00	2.40	1.80	1.20	.80	Qt.	2.50
	1000	....	....	20.00	16.00	12.00	7.00	Pk.	18.00
Mrs. H. A. Caesar....	1	.20	.15	.10	....	....	....	Pkg.	.15
	10	1.60	1.20	.80	.60	.40	.30	1000	1.50
	100	....	9.00	7.00	5.00	3.50	2.50	Qt.	5.00
Mrs. J. A. Walsh.....	1	.10	.08	.07	....	....	....	Pkg.	.10
	10	.80	.65	.55	....	....	....	1000	1.00
	100	5.00	4.00	3.00	....	....	....		
Mrs. L. S. Schweppe..	1	.10	.08	.07	....	....	....	Pkg.	.10
	10	.60	.50	.40	....	....	....	1000	75
	100	....	4.00	3.00	2.00	....	....	Qt.	1.50
Mrs. Leon Douglas...	1	.10	.08	.07	....	....	....	Pkg.	.10
	10	.80	.70	.60	.45	.35	.25	1000	1.00
	100	....	4.00	3.00	2.00	1.25	.75	Qt.	3.50
	1000	....	36.00	24.00	16.00	10.00	6.00	....	....
Mrs. Paul Dieball....	1	....	....	.30	.20	.15	.10	1	.10
Mrs. P. W. Sisson....	1	.40	.30	.20	.15	.10	....	Pkg.	.25
	10	3.20	2.40	1.60	1.20	80	.50	1000	3.00
	100	16.00	12.00	8.00	6.00	4.00	2.50	Qt.	10.00
	1000	....	90.00	65.00	50.00	30.00	15.00	Pk.	60.00
Mrs. T. Rattray.....	1	1.50	1.25	1.00	....	....	....	....	....
Mrs. S. A. Errey.....	1	4.00	3.00	2.00	....	1.25	....	10	1.00
Mrs. Stanleigh Arnold	8	.50	.40	.30	.20	.15	.10	10	.25
	10	4.00	3.20	2.40	1.60	1.20	.80	....	....
Mrs. Van Konynenburg	1	.60	.50	.40	.30	.20	.10	Pkg.	.25
	10	4.80	4.00	3.20	2.40	1.60	.80	100	1.50
	100	25.00	20.00	15.00	12.00	9.00	6.00	1000	12.00
	1000	....	150.00	120.00	90.00	75.00	40.00	Qt.	25.00
Mrs. Walter Lytton..	1	....	....	....	.75	.50	.35	1	.15
Mrs. W. Richardson..	1	.10	.08	.07	....	....	....	Pkg.	.10
	10	.70	.60	.50	·.40	.30	.20	1000	.75
	100	5.00	4.00	3.00	2.00	1.00	.75	Qt.	1.50
	1000	40.00	32.00	24.00	16.00	8.00	6.00	Pk.	9.00
Nancy Hanks........	1	.20	.15	.10	....	....	....	Pkg.	.20
	10	1.00	.80	.60	.50	.40	.30	100	.50
	100	6.00	5.00	3.00	2.00	1.25	.75	1000	2.00
O. A. D. Baldwin....	1	....	....	2.00	1.50	1.00	.75	5	1.00
Obelisque..........	1	.25	.20	.15	....	....	....	Pkg.	.25
	10	2.00	1.60	1.20	....	....	....	1000	1.50
October............	1	1.50	1.25	1.00	.75	.50	.35	1	.15
Olive Goodrich.......	1	.30	.25	.20	.15	.10	....	Pkg.	.30
	10	2.40	2.00	1.60	1.20	.80	.50	1000	10.00
	100	18.00	15.00	12.00	9.00	5.00	3.00	Qt.	25.00
	1000	....	....	....	70.00	40.00	20.00	....	....
Opalescent..........	1	.10	.08	.07	....	....	....	Pkg.	.10
	10	.65	.55	.45	.35	.25	.15	1000	1.00
	100	4.00	3.50	3.00	2.00	·1.00	.60	Qt.	2.50
	1000	30.00	25.00	20.00	15.00	8.00	4.50	Pk.	10.00

8

	Per	No. 1	No. 2	No. 3	No. 4	No. 5	No. 6	Bulblets Per	
Oraflame	1	1.25	1.00	.75	.45	.35	.20	10	.50
	10	10.00	8.00	6.00	3.50	2.50	1.50	100	3.50
	100	80.00	64.00	36.00	27.00	20.00	12.00	1000	25.00
Orange Fire	1	----	----	1.00	.75	.50	.35	1	.15
Orange Flame	1	.15	.12	.10	----	----	----	Pkg.	.15
	10	1.20	.90	.70	.50	.35	.25	1000	1.00
	100	9.00	6.00	4.00	3.00	2.00	1.00	Qt.	4.00
	1000	----	54.00	36.00	27.00	18.00	9.00	----	----
Orange Gold	1	----	----	1.00	.75	.50	.35	1	.15
Orange Wonder	1	1.25	1.00	.75	.45	.35	.20	10	.50
	10	10.00	8.00	6.00	3.50	2.50	1.50	100	3.50
	100	----	64.00	36.00	----	20.00	12.00	1000	25.00
Orchid Lady	1	1.00	.80	.60	.50	.40	.30	10	.60
	10	8.00	6.00	5.00	4.00	3.00	2.00	100	4.00
Osalin	1	.15	.12	.10	----	----	----	Pkg.	.15
	10	1.00	.90	.80	.60	.40	.30	100	1.00
	100	7.00	6.00	5.00	4.00	2.50	1.25	1000	1.75
	1000	----	45.00	40.00	32.00	20.00	10.00	Qt.	7.00
Pasadena	1	.15	.12	.10	----	----	----	Pkg.	.15
	10	----	1.00	.80	.60	.40	.25	1000	1.00
	100	----	4.00	3.00	2.20	1.40	1.00	----	----
Pauline Kunderd	1	5.00	4.00	3.00	2.50	2.00	1.00	Each	.50
Paul Pfitzer	1	.50	.40	.30	.25	.20	.15	Pkg.	.25
	10	4.00	3.50	2.50	2.00	1.50	1.00	100	1.75
	100	35.00	25.00	20.00	15.00	12.00	8.00	1000	15.00
	1000	250.00	200.00	160.00	120.00	90.00	60.00	Qt.	40.00
Peace	1	.10	.08	.07	----	----	----	Pkg.	.10
	10	.60	.50	.40	.30	.20	.15	1000	.75
	100	----	3.00	2.00	1.50	1.00	.75	....	----
Pearl of California	1	.70	.60	.50	.40	.30	.20	10	.40
	10	5.50	4.50	3.50	2.50	2.00	1.50	100	2.40
	100	40.00	30.00	20.00	15.00	12.00	10.00	1000	20.00
	1000	300.00	240.00	150.00	100.00	75.00	60.00	Qt.	75.00
Persia	1	.10	.08	.07	----	----	----	Pkg.	.10
	10	.70	.60	.50	.40	.30	.20	1000	1.00
	100	6.00	5.00	4.00	3.00	2.00	1.00	Qt.	4.00
	1000	----	40.00	32.00	24.00	----	----	Pk.	20.00
Pfitzer's Fortuna	1	.50	.40	.30	.25	.20	.15	2	.10
	10	4.00	3.20	2.40	2.00	1.60	.80	100	3.00
Pfitzer's Triumph	1	.65	.55	.45	----	----	----	10	.40
	10	5.25	4.50	3.75	----	----	----	100	2.50
Phaenomen	1	.20	.15	.10	----	----	----	Pkg.	.15
	10	1.50	1.20	.90	.70	.50	.30	1000	3.00
	100	12.00	10.00	8.00	6.00	4.00	2.50	Qt.	10.00
	1000	80.00	65.00	45.00	30.00	20.00	12.00	Pk.	50.00
Philatelia	1	1.50	1.25	1.00	.75	.50	.25	1	.15
Philip Breitmeyer	1	1.00	.80	.60	.40	.30	.20	1	.10
Pink Cloud	1	.20	.15	.10	----	----	----	Pkg.	.25
	10	1.60	1.20	.80	----	----	----	----	----
Pink Delight	1	----	1.25	1.00	.75	.50	.25	10	.75
Pink Enchantor	1	----	----	----	.75	.50	.35	1	.15
Pink Lily	1	.10	.08	.07	----	----	----	Pkg.	.10
	10	----	.60	.50	.40	.30	.20	1000	1.00
	100	----	3.50	2.75	2.00	----	----	Qt.	2.00
Pompeian Beauty	1	.30	.25	.20	.15	.10	----	Pkg.	.25
	10	2.40	2.00	1.60	1.20	.80	.50	1000	2.00
Pond Lily	1	----	----	1.00	.75	.50	.35	1	.15
Pres. Harding	1	.15	.12	10	----	----	----	Pkg.	.15
	10	1.20	.90	.60	.40	.25	.15	1000	1.00
	100	6.00	5.00	4.00	3.00	2.00	1.00	Qt.	3.00
	1000	50.00	40.00	32.00	24.00	15.00	7.00	Pk.	15.00

	Per	No. 1	No. 2	No. 3	No. 4	No. 5	No. 6	Bulblets Per	
Pres. Lincoln	1	....	....	4.00	3.00	2.00	1.00	1	.50
Pretty Pink	1	....	1.25	1.00	.75	.50	.35	1	.15
Pride of Oregon	1	5.00	4.00	3.00	2.00	1.00	.75	1	.50
Pride of Portland	1	3.00	2.50	2.00	1.50	1.00	.75	1	.40
Pride of Wanakah	1	.20	.15	.12	.10	....	....	Pkg.	.15
	10	1.50	1.20	.95	.80	.60	.40	1000	1.00
	100	....	....	5.00	3.00	2.00	1.25	Qt.	4.00
Primrose Princess	1	.75	.60	.50	.35	.25	.20	Pkg	.50
	10	3.50	2.50	1.50	1.00	.75	.50	100	1.00
	100	20.00	17.50	15.00	10.00	8.00	5.00	1000	5.00
Prince of India	1	.25	.20	.15	.10	....	....	Pkg.	.25
	10	2.00	1.60	1.20	.80	.60	.50		
Purest of All	1	.25	.20	.15	.10	....	....	Pkg.	.25
	10	2.00	1.50	1.20	.80	.60	.40	1000	1.00
	100	10.00	8.00	6.00	4.00	2.75	1.50	Qt.	4.00
	1000	80.00	60.00	50.00	35.00	30.00	12.00		
Purple Glory	1	.10	.08	.07	....	....	....	Pkg.	.10
	10	.70	.60	.50	.40	.30	.20	1000	1.00
	100	6.00	5.00	2.75	2.00	1.50	....	Qt.	2.50
	1000	50.00	40.00	25.00	16.00	12.00	....		
Purple Progress	1	....	5.00	4.00	3.00	2.00	1.00	1	.50
Purple Queen	1	.25	.20	.15	.10	....	....	Pkg.	.25
	10	2.00	1.60	1.20	.80	.60	.40	1000	2.00
	100	12.00	10.00	8.00	6.00	4.00	2.50		
Queen Mary	1	....	....	.25	.20	.15	.10	10	.35
	10	....	....	2.00	1.60	1.20	.80	100	3.00
Quinton	1	.10	.08	.07	....	....	....	Pkg.	.10
	10	.60	.50	.40	.30	.20	.10	1000	1.00
	100	4.00	3.20	2.50	1.50	1.00	.50	Qt.	2.00
	1000	30.00	25.00	20.00	12.00	8.00	4.00	Pk.	10.00
Radiant Orange	1	.75	.65	.55	.45	.35	.25	1	.15
Radiant Queen	1	.50	.40	.30	.25	.20	.15	Pkg.	.15
Ravenna	1	....	....	.60	.40	.30	.20	1	.10
Reah	1	.35	.30	.25	.20	.15	.10	Pkg.	.35
	10	2.50	2.00	1.50	1.00	.75	.50	1000	3.50
	100	17.50	15.00	12.50	10.00	8.00	6.00	Qt.	6.00
Red Fire	1	.10	.08	.07	....	....	....	Pkg.	.10
	10	.70	.60	.50	.40	.30	.20	1000	.80
	100	4.00	3.00	2.40	1.80	1.20	.80	Qt.	2.50
Red Glory	1	....	....	.50	.40	.30	.20	10	1.00
Red Splendor	1	1.00	.80	.60	.40	....	....	1	.15
Red Tornado	1	5.00	4.00	3.00	2.00	1.25	.75	1	.40
	10	40.00	32.00	24.00	16.00	10.00	6.00	10	2.50
Red Velvet	1	....	....	.35	.25	.20	.15	Pkg.	.25
Reflection	1	.25	.20	.15	.10	....	....	Pkg.	.20
	10	....	....	1.20	.80	.60	.40	1000	5.00
Remarkable	1	.75	.65	.55	.45	.35	.25	10	.50
	10	6.00	5.00	4.00	3.00	2.00	1.25	100	3.00
Renown	1	.50	.30	.30	....	....	....	....	....
Resplendent	1	1.00	.80	.60	.40	.30	.20	10	.50
	10	8.00	6.00	4.00	3.00	2.00	1.25	100	2.00
Rev. Ewbank	1	.10	.08	.07	....	....	....	Pkg.	.10
	10	.65	.55	.45	.35	.25	.15	1000	1.00
	100	....	3.00	2.40	1.80	1.20	.75	Qt.	3.00
	1000	....	25.00	22.00	16.00	8.00	6.00		
Richard Diener	1	.10	.08	.07	....	....	....	Pkg.	.10
	10	.65	.55	.45	.35	.25	.15	1000	1.00
	100	3.50	3.00	2.50	2.00	1.50	1.00	Qt.	3.00
	1000	30.00	25.00	20.00	15.00	10.00	6.00	Pk.	15.00

	Per	No. 1	No. 2	No. 3	No. 4	No. 5	No. 6	BULBLETS Per	
Rippling Waters	1	3.00	2.50	2.00	1.50	1.00	.75	1	.25
Rita Beck..........	1	.75	.60	.40	.30	.25	.20	10	.30
	10	6.00	5.00	3.60	2.40	2.00	1.60	100	2.50
	100	45.00	35.00	25.00	20.00	16.00	12.00	1000	25.00
R. J. Kunderd.......	1	.10	.08	.07	....	....	....	Pkg.	.10
	10	.80	.70	.50	.40	.30	.25	100	25
	100	....	4.00	3.00	2.20	1.40	1.00	1000	1.00
Roderick Dhu.......	1	1.00	.80	.60	.40	.30	.20	Pkg.	.50
	10	8.00	6.00	4.00	3.00	2.00	1.25	1000	40.00
Romance...........	1	.10	.08	.07	....	....	....	Pkg.	.10
	10	.60	.50	.40	.30	.20	.10	1000	.75
	100	4.00	3.00	2.40	1.50	1.00	.60	Qt.	2.00
	1000	35.00	28.00	20.00	12.00	8.00	4.50	Pk.	10.00
Rose Ash...........	1	.10	.08	.07	....	....	....	Pkg.	.10
	10	.60	.50	.40	.30	.20	.10	1000	1.00
	100	4.00	3.50	3.00	2.50	1.50	1.00	Qt.	2.50
Rose Mulberry.......	1	.15	.12	.10	....	....	....	Pkg.	.25
	10	1.20	1.00	.80	.60	.40	.30	1000	3.00
	100	....	....	6.50	5.00	3.00	2.00	....	....
Royal Lavender......	1	1.50	1.25	1.00	.75	.50	.35	No bbts.	
	10	12.00	10.00	8.00	6.00	4.00	2.75	....	....
	100	100.00	80.00	60.00	45.00	30.00	20.00	....	....
	1000	....	....	400.00	300.00	225.00	150.00	....	....
Royal Purple........	1	.50	.40	.30	.20	.15	.10	Pkg.	.25
Rudolph Valentino...	1	1.00	.80	.60	.40	.30	.20	Pkg.	.50
	10	8.00	6.00	4.00	3.00	2.00	1.00	1000	3.00
Ruffled Gold........	1	2.00	1.50	1.00	.75	.50	.25	Pkg.	.40
	10	16.00	12.00	8.00	6.00	4.00	2.00	100	2.00
	100	80.00	75.00	50.00	35.00	20.00	12.00	1000	15.00
	1000	....	....	....	200.00	150.00	75.00	Qt.	35.00
Sacajawea or Smoky..	1	.25	.20	.15	.10	....	....	Pkg.	.25
	10	2.00	1.60	1.20	.80	.50	.30	1000	2.00
	100	12.00	10.00	8.00	6.00	4.00	2.00	Qt.	5.00
St. Thomas.........	1	.15	.12	.10	....	....	....	Pkg.	.15
	10	1.20	.90	.70	.50	.35	.20	1000	1.00
	100	6.00	5.00	4.00	3.00	2.00	1.00	Qt.	3.00
	1000	45.00	35.00	25.00	18.00	12.00	8.00	Pk.	15.00
Salbach's Pink.......	1	5.00	4.50	3.50	2.00	1.50	1.00	1	.35
Saraband...........	1	.25	.20	.15	.10	....	....	Pkg.	.25
	10	1.60	1.20	.90	.60	.35	.20	1000	2.00
	100	12.50	10.00	8.00	6.00	4.00	2.50	Qt.	5.00
Scarlet King........	1	....	....	2.00	1.50	1.00	.75	1	.25
Scarlet Princeps......	1	.10	.08	.07	....	....	....	Pkg.	.10
	10	.70	.60	.50	.40	.30	.20	1000	1.00
	100	....	3.50	2.50	2.00	1.50	1.00	Qt.	2.00
Scarlet Wonder......	1	.10	.08	.07	....	....	....	Pkg.	.10
	10	.60	.50	.40	.30	.20	.10	1000	.75
	100	3.60	3.00	2.40	1.50	1.00	.70	Qt.	1.75
	1000	....	25.00	20.00	12.00	8.00	5.00	....	....
Senorita............	1	....	1.25	1.00	.75	.50	.35	10	.60
	10	....	....	6.00	5.00	4.00	3.00	100	5.00
Sidney Plummer.....	1	....	.10	.07	....	....	....	Pkg.	.10
	10	....	.60	.50	.40	.30	.20	1000	.75
	100	....	4.00	3.00	2.20	1.40	.75	Qt.	1.75
	1000	....	32.00	25.00	18.00	10.00	5.00	Pk.	12.00
Sir Thomas Lipton...	1	....	....	1.00	.75	.50	....	1	.10
Smoke.............	1	....	.10	.07	....	....	....	Pkg.	.10
	10	....	.80	.55	.35	.25	.15	1000	1.00
	100	....	5.00	4.00	3.00	2.00	1.00	Qt.	2.50
Star of the Sea.......	1	1.00	.80	.60	.50	.40	.30	Pkg.	.50

11

Name	Per	No. 1	No. 2	No. 3	No. 4	No. 5	No. 6	Bulblets Per	
Stuttgardia	1	4.00	3.50	3.00	....	....	....	1	.40
Sulphur Frills	1	.10	.08	.07	....	....	....	Pkg.	.10
	10	.80	.60	.50	.40	.30	.20	1000	1.50
	100	6.00	5.00	4.00	3.00	2.00	1.25	Qt.	3.00
Sultan	1	10.00	8.75	7.50	6.25	5.00	3.75	1	1.00
Sweet Rose	1	.25	.20	.15	....	....	....	Pkg.	.25
	10	2.00	1.60	1.20	....	....	....	100	.50
	100	10.00	8.00	6.50	....	....	....	1000	3.00
	1000	....	65.00	50.00	....	....	....	Qt.	6.00
Sword of Mahomet	1	.50	.40	.30	.25	.20	.15	10	.40
	10	4.00	3.20	2.40	2.00	16.0	1.00	100	3.00
Taro	1	.10	.08	.07	....	....	....	Pkg.	.10
	10	.70	.60	.40	.30	.20	.15	1000	1.00
	100	5.00	4.00	3.00	2.00	1.00	.60	Qt.	2.50
	1000	40.00	32.00	24.00	16.00	8.00	4.50	Pk.	12.00
Thais Valdemar	1	.15	.12	.10	....	....	....	Pkg.	.15
	10	....	1.00	.80	.60	.40	.25	1000	1.50
	100	....	8.00	6.00	4.00	2.50	1.25	....	....
The President	1	.20	.15	.10	....	....	....	Pkg.	.15
	10	1.60	1.20	.80	.60	.40	.20	1000	1.50
Thistle	1	.10	.08	.07	....	....	....	Pkg.	.10
	10	.70	.60	.50	....	....	....	1000	1.00
	100	....	3.50	2.50	....	....	....	....	....
Thos. T. Kent	1	....	.10	.07	....	....	....	Pkg.	.10
	10	....	.60	.50	....	.30	.20	1000	1.00
	100	....	4.00	3.00	....	1.50	1.00	....	....
Thos. A. Edison	1	....	4.00	3.00	2.00	1.00	.75	1	.50
Tiger	1	....	....	.20	.15	.10	....	Pkg.	.25
	10	....	....	1.60	1.20	.80	.60	1000	2.00
Titan	1	.40	.30	.20	.15	.10	....	Pkg.	.25
	10	3.50	2.40	1.60	1.20	.80	.50	1000	2.00
Tobersun	1	2.00	1.75	1.50	1.25	1.00	.75	1	.20
	10	16.00	14.00	12.00	10.00	8.00	6.00	10	1.60
	100	....	....	90.00	70.00	50.00	40.00	100	10.00
Troubadour	1	1.25	1.00	.75	.50	....	....	1	.15
Twilight	1	.10	.08	.07	....	....	....	Pkg.	.10
	10	.70	.60	.50	....	....	....	1000	1.00
	100	5.00	4.00	3.00	....	....	....	....	....
Tycko Zang	1	.10	.08	.07	....	....	....	Pkg.	.10
	10	.70	.60	.50	.40	.25	.15	1000	1.00
	100	5.00	4.00	2.50	1.50	1.00	.75	Qt.	3.00
	1000	40.00	32.00	20.00	12.00	9.00	6.00	Pk.	18.00
Veilchenblau	1	.60	.50	.40	.30	.20	.15	Pkg.	.30
	10	4.50	4.00	3.00	2.40	1.60	1.00	100	2.40
	100	40.00	30.00	20.00	....	12.00	8.00	1000	20.00
Veiled Brillance	1	.45	.35	.25	.20	.15	.10	Pkg.	.30
	10	3.50	2.50	1.75	1.60	1.00	.60	100	1.00
Velvet Diamond	1	1.50	1.25	1.00	.75	.50	.25	2	.25
Violet Prince	1	.25	.20	.15	.10	....	....	Pkg.	.25
	10	2.00	1.60	1.20	.80	.60	.40	1000	2.00
Waban	1	.25	.20	.15	.10	....	....	Pkg.	.25
	10	2.00	1.50	1.20	.80	.60	.40	100	2.00
	100	....	12.00	10.00	7.00	5.00	3.00	1000	15.00
Wawasee	1	.25	.20	.15	.10	....	....	Pkg.	.25
	10	2.00	1.60	1.20	.80	.50	.25	1000	2.00
Wedgewood	1	.50	.40	.30	.20	.15	.10	10	1.50
W. H. Phipps	1	.20	.15	.10	....	....	....	Pkg.	.20
	10	1.60	1.20	.80	....	....	....	1000	2.50
W. G. Badger	1	.10	.08	.07	....	....	....	Pkg.	.10
	10	.80	.70	.60	.50	.40	.30	1000	1.00
	100	4.50	3.40	2.70	2.00	1.40	1.00	Qt.	3.50

	Per	No. 1	No. 2	No. 3	No. 4	No. 5	No. 6	BULBLETS Per	
Wodan	1	6.00	5.50	5.00	....	....	....	1	1.00
Yellow Perfection	1	3.00	2.50	2.00	....	....	....	1	.25

PRIMULINUS

	Per	No. 1	No. 2	No. 3	No. 4	No. 5	No. 6	BULBLETS Per	
Ada De Poy	1	.15	.12	.10	....	....	....	Pkg.	.10
	10	1.00	.80	.60	.50	.35	.25	1000	1.00
Aflame	1	1.00	.80	.60	.50	.40	.30	10	.60
	10	7.50	6.25	5.00	4.00	3.00	2.40	100	2.50
	100	50.00	40.00	32.00	....	18.00	12.00	1000	20.00
Apricot Glow	1	.50	.40	.30	.20	.10	.07	10	.40
	10	4.00	3.20	2.40	1.60	.80	.55	100	1.25
	100	32.00	25.00	19.00	12.00	6.40	4.40	1000	10.00
	1000	....	....	150.00	100.00	50.00	30.00	Qt.	20.00
Cara Mia	1	2.00	1.50	1.00	.75	.50	.35	10	1.25
	10	16.00	12.00	8.00	6.00	4.00	2.50	100	10.00
	100	120.00	90.00	60.00	45.00	30.00	20.00	1000	80.00
Copper Bronze	1	.20	.15	.10	....	....	....	Pkg.	.20
	10	1.50	1.20	.80	.50	.30	.20	1000	1.20
	100	10.00	8.00	6.00	4.40	3.60	2.50	Qt.	3.00
	1000	80.00	60.00	45.00	35.00	20.00	15.00	Pk.	20.00
Copper Gold	1	2.50	2.00	1.50	1.00	.75	.50	1	.25
E. B. Williamson	1	.10	.08	.07	....	....	....	Pkg.	.10
	10	.60	.50	.40	.30	.20	.15	1000	1.00
	100	5.00	4.00	3.00	2.00	1.25	.75	Qt.	2.00
	1000	40.00	32.00	24.00	15.00	10.00	6.00	Pk.	10.00
Enchantress	1	.15	.12	.10	....	....	....	Pkg.	.15
	10	1.00	.80	.60	.40	.30	.20	1000	1.00
	100	8.00	6.00	5.00	3.00	2.00	1.25	Qt.,	2.00
Ethelyn	1	.15	.12	.10	....	....	....	Pkg.	.15
	10	1.00	.80	.60	.45	.35	.25	1000	1.00
	100	.6.00	5.00	4.00	2.75	1.40	1.00	Qt.	3.00
Evening	1	.25	.20	.15	.10	....	....	Pkg.	.20
	10	2.00	1.60	1.20	.80	.50	.25	1000	2.00
	100	....	10.00	8.00	6.00	4.00	2.00	....	....
Firy Knight	1	.15	.12	.10	....	....	....	Pkg.	.15
	10	1.20	.90	.70	.55	.40	.25	1000	1.50
	100	....	....	5.00	4.00	3.00	2 00	....	....
Golden Frills	1	.25	.20	.15	.10	....	....	Pkg.	.25
	10	2.00	1.60	1.20	.80	.45	.25	1000	2.00
	100	12.00	10.00	6.00	4.75	3.00	2.00	Qt.	6.50
	1000	100.00	80.00	50.00	35.00	20.00	10.00	Pk.	40.00
Golden Orange	1	.75	.60	.50	.40	.30	.20	10	.50
Goldielocks	1	.50	.40	.30	.20	.15	.10	Pkg.	.50
	10	4.00	3.20	2.40	1.60	1.20	.80	1000	30.00
	100	30.00	25.00	20.00	14.00	10.00	7.00	....	....
Harbinger	1	.20	.15	.10	....	....	....	Pkg.	.20
	10	1.50	1.20	.80	.60	.45	.30	1000	2.00
	100	10.00	8.00	6.00	5.00	3.50	2.00	Qt.	4.00
Improved Tiplady	1	.25	.20	.15	.10	....	....	Pkg.	.25
	10	1.00	.90	.80	.60	.40	.30	1000	5.00
	100	7.50	7 00	6.00	5.00	3.00	2.00	....	....
King of Oranges	1	.30	.25	.20	.15	....	....	Pkg.	.30
	10	2.40	2.00	1.60	1.20	.80	.50	100	2.00
Kund's Yellow Beauty	1	.10	.08	.07	....	....	....	Pkg.	.10
	10	.70	.60	.50	.40	.30	.20	1000	1.00

13

	Per	No. 1	No. 2	No. 3	No. 4	No. 5	No. 6	BULBLETS Per	
Marigold	1	.30	.25	.20	.15	.10	--------	Pkg.	.25
	10	2.00	1.60	1.20	.80	.60	.40	1000	2.00
Mongolia	1	.50	.40	.30	.25	.20	.15	2	.10
Mrs. Calvin Coolidge	1	1.50	1.25	1.00	.75	.50	.30	1	.15
	10	10.00	8.00	6.00	4.50	3.00	2.00	100	10.00
	100	80.00	60.00	45.00	30.00	20.00	15.00	1000	70.00
Oneta	1	.50	.40	.30	.25	.20	.15	1	.10
	10	4.00	3.00	2.25	1.50	1.00	--------	100	7.00
Orange Butterfly	1	1.50	1.25	1.00	.75	.50	.35	1	.15
	10	7.50	6.50	4.00	3.00	2.00	1.00	100	3.00
	100	50.00	45.00	30.00	25.00	15.00	8.00	1000	20.00
Orange Queen	1	.10	.08	.07	--------	--------	--------	Pkg.	.10
	10	.60	.50	.40	.30	.20	.10	1000	1.00
	100	4.00	3.00	2.40	1.50	1.00	.75	Qt.	3.00
	1000	--------	25.00	18.00	12.00	8.00	6.00	Pk.	15.00
Pansy	1	.10	.08	.07	--------	--------	--------	Pkg.	.10
	10	.70	.60	.50	.40	.30	.20	1000	1.00
	100	6.00	5.00	4.00	3.00	2.00	1.00	Qt.	2.50
Patricia Carter	1	.75	.60	.50	.40	.30	.20	1	.10
	10	6.00	5.00	4.00	3.00	2.00	1.25	10	.50
Queen of Orange	1	.30	.25	.20	.15	.10	--------	Pkg.	.25
	10	2.40	2.00	1.60	1.20	.80	.50	1000	2.00
	100	15 00	12.00	9.00	7.00	5.00	3.00	Qt.	4.00
Rose Mist	1	.20	.15	.10	--------	--------	--------	Pkg.	.20
	10	1.50	1.20	.90	.70	.50	.35	1000	3.00
	100	12.00	10.00	8.00	6.00	4.00	2.00	Qt.	10.00
	1000	90.00	70.00	50.00	40.00	30.00	15.00		
Salmon Glow	1	.10	.08	.07	--------	--------	--------	Pkg.	.10
	10	.80	.60	.50	.40	.30	.20	1000	1.00
	100	4.50	4.00	3.00	2.00	1.00	.75	Qt.	2.00
	1000	30.00	25.00	20.00	15.00	10.00	7.00	Pk.	10.00
Scarlet Bedder	1	.25	.20	.15	.10	--------	--------	Pkg.	.30
	10	1.50	1.25	1.00	.80	.60	.50	1000	3.00
	100	12.00	10.00	8.00	6.00	5.00	4.00		
Sweeter Seventeen	1	.50	.40	.30	.20	.15	.10	Pkg.	.25
	10	3.50	2.50	2.00	1.50	1.00	.60	1000	3.00
Taurus	1	.10	.08	.07	--------	--------	--------	Pkg.	.10
	10	.70	.60	.50	.40	.30	.20	1000	1.00
	100	5.00	4.00	3.00	2.00	1.00	.60	Qt.	2.00
Temblor	1	.15	.12	.10	--------	--------	--------	Pkg.	.15
	10	1.00	.80	.60	.50	.40	.25	1000	1.00
The Orchid	1	.60	.50	.40	.30	.20	.15	Pkg.	.25
	10	5.00	4.00	3.00	2.00	1.50	1.00	100	1.20
	100	40.00	32.00	24.00	16.00	10.00	6.00	1000	10.00
Winifred	1	.50	.40	.30	.20	.15	.10	Pkg.	.50
	10	4.00	3.20	2.40	1.60	1.20	.80	1000	30.00
	100	30.00	25.00	20.00	14.00	10.00	8.00		
Virginia Lou	1	.10	.08	.07	--------	--------	--------	Pkg.	.10
	10	.70	.60	.50	.40	.30	.20	1000	1.00
Zona	1	.25	.20	.15	.10	--------	--------	Pkg.	.25
	10	2.00	1.60	1.20	.80	.60	.40	1000	2.50
	100	12.00	10.00	8.00	6.00	4.00	2.50	Qt.	5.00

My bulbs this year are positively the finest I have ever had, plump, high crowned, and healthy. By disinfecting everything I plant and planting on new ground every year I have practically gotten away from disease entirely. One of my customers writing in for my new price list says "your bulbs speak for themselves."

Those who have bought of me before know that I will treat them right on price and quantity and quality. To those who have not bought of me I want to say "just give me a trial order. I think I can make you a permanent customer.

MIXTURES. I do not advise an advanced amateur ever to buy a mixture of glads. And they usually will not. It is so much more fun to keep the kinds separate and learn to know them all by name, learn the different characteristics of the various varieties. Then if there is one you especially like and you want to get more you know what it is you want.

But there are thousands of people who have gardens, who want a few glads and have not yet got the "bug," and so do not want to bother with keeping the kinds separate. For these people I have a mixture that is especially good. It contains at least thirty varieties, good ones in many different shades. These are mixed as the orders come in, so if you prefer more of one shade and less of others I can mix them that way. If you do not like reds I can leave them out and the same with other colors. If you leave it to me I will give you a fine assortment of at least thirty kinds in the collections of 50 or more bulbs. Bulbs are at least 1 inch in diameter and not the little ½ inch bulbs sent out in many collections.

THIS IS MY NO. 1 COLLECTION.
They are priced at $3.00 for 100 bulbs, prepaid. $1.75 for 50 or $1.00 for 25, all prepaid. Next fall if you want your money back just say so. **I don't believe there is as good a mixture offered by any other grower in the country at anywhere near the price.**
I have had many wonderful reports from the collections I sent out last year.

I also have a **NO. 2 COLLECTION** at the same price. This includes only primulinus varieties.

NO. 3 COLLECTION $5.00 per 100, 50 and 25 at the 100 rate. This includes at least 40 varieties in many different shades and several of the newer varieties.

NO. 4 COLLECTION $10.00 per 100, 50 and 25 at the 100 rate. This contains at least 50 varieties including many of the finest exhibition varieties and is sure to please anyone. If labeled these collections would cost a great deal more.

Certain varieties are included in all the mixtures but in the higher priced ones are some varieties that are exceptionally fine and of an exhibition quality. All are very well worth the money. I am not afraid to compare them with any collection in the country.

But remember the varieties in the collections are not labeled.

Mixed bulblets	1000	$ .50
	Quart	1.50

These contain many fine varieties.

Join the **A. G. S.,** $2.00 a year. You get the "Gladiolus Review" a monthly magazine devoted solely to gladiolus. I also give a bulb of Copper Bronze and one of Golden Frills with each new member.

Join the New England Gladiolus Society. $1.00 a year. You will receive the year book for 1929 and the one for 1930. These are fine illustrated books of about 100 pages. Send me the money and I will attend to it for you.

"The glads "Lorice" you sent me have bloomed and I am perfectly delighted with them."   Mrs. W. N. H., Warrenton, Va.

"Marmora is all you claimed. A wonderful spike and of the most beautiful color. 5 feet tall. 19 buds with 9 open at once. Other spikes as good. Emile Aubrun in every way a companion of Marmora except the color. That is splendid too. Royal Lavender had only two blooming bulbs but they are fine. The color very beautiful, size good and in every way one that I will want to keep. Rose Mist, dainty and beautiful. Attracts the admiration of all. Gloriana, the color so soft and glowing and the peculiar opening of the buds so attractive that it is in a class by itself. Marnia, beautiful color but stems somewhat crooked. That can be overlooked as it more than makes up in other ways. Golden Dream, Annie Laurie and Dr. Nelson Shook all good.

Every one which were suggested by you are more than satisfactory and will have a place in my garden again next year."   W. B. R., Peoria, Ill.

Dear Sir: I ordered bulbs from you last year and was greatly pleased with results. Yours were the only ones I ordered that every one grew, and every one bloomed, and best of all **every one was true to name,** and I got bulbs from several firms. And most of my bulbs from you were size 5 and 6.

Mrs. **L. H.**, Allen Grove, Wis.

16

MRS. F. C. HORNBERGER. (HORNBERGER) Large white with no markings. Several open. A fine exhibition variety as well as commercial. Winner at many shows. Late.

MRS. F. C. PETERS. (FISCHER) Very beautiful orchid lavender with darker blotch. Many blooms open. Tall, straight stem. The finest commercial, late lavender and a top notch exhibition variety.

MRS. H. A. CAESAR. (VAUGHAN) Fine light lavender. In the house this fades to a wonderfully beautiful clear shade. Several open on nice spike.

MRS. J. R. WALSH. (D) Large ruffled flesh pink with flame red blotch covering nearly the whole of the 3 lower petals. Very long spike. Fine.

MRS. L. S. SCHWEPPE. (K) Deep peach blossom with velvety red blotches. Not large but beautiful and distinct. Several open. Stands frost well.

MRS. LEON DOUGLAS. (D) Salmon-rose striped with flame and scarlet. A real wonder glad. About the tallest, largest and showiest glad in existence. Several immense blooms open at a time. Have had tip blooms over 5 inches across. One of the leaders at the shows and becoming very popular as a cut flower.

MRS. PAUL DIEBALL. (K) Deep salmon pink with darker throat.

MRS. P. W. SISSON. (COLEMAN) Creamy light pink. Tall strong grower Several large beautiful blooms open at a time. A fine outstanding variety, one of my favorites. Will be grown by the million.

MRS. T. RATTRAY. (ERREY) Bright rose. Very long spike with nearly all open at once. Fine for exhibition.

MRS. S. A. ERREY. (ERREY) Very large orange with orange red blotch. Several immense blooms open. Fades some in the sun.

MRS. STANLEIGH ARNOLD. (D) Soft phlox pink striped with light purple. Long spikes nearly all open at once. Fine exhibition variety. Odd but pretty.

MRS. VAN KONYNENBURG. (PF.) Tall, clear, medium light blue. Several open. The best in its shade of blue. A big seller.

MRS. WALTER LYTTON. (K) Deep salmon flesh with creamy throat.

MRS. WILLARD RICHARDSON. (D) Early dark red. Tall strong grower. A fine dark red glad too little known.

NANCY HANKS. (SALBACH) Apricot shading to orange pink. Red marking on lip. Several large well placed blooms open. Very distinctive and showy.

O. A. D. BALDWIN. (SALBACH) Deep velvety red with darker blotch. Several well placed blooms open.

OBELISQUE. (HOLLAND) Very large cream yellow with darker yellow lip. Several open. Fine for the garden or exhibition.

OCTOBER. (K) Very large beautiful deep old rose flaked darker. Very fine.

OLIVE GOODRICH. (GOODRICH) White shading to pink at edges. Pale yellow throat. Several open. Tall strong plant with long spike. This is a fine commercial and will be grown in quantity when available. If you grow for cut flowers be sure to try this.

OPALESCENT. (BILL) Pale lavender with darker lines in the throat. Fine commercial. Nice easy grower.

ORAFLAME. (KEMP) Light orange shading to a golden throat. Several open. Tall, straight plant. Very beautiful color. You should try it.

ORANGE FIRE. (K) Ruffled orange red, medium size. Fiery color.

ORANGE FLAME. (K) Orange scarlet shading lighter toward upper center. Small velvety purplish spot on flame orange lip. Heavily ruffled. This variety is not so well known as it should be as it is one of the very finest glads in existence. Very distinctive and beautiful. Late.

ORANGE GOLD. (K) Deep orange red. Very showy.

17

ORANGE WONDER. (Kemp) Clear deep orange. Large flowers. Tall, strong, straight plant. Very good.

ORCHID LADY. (Spencer) Very large orchid lavender. Well liked by the florists.

OSALIN. (Salbach) Coral pink with soft orange shading in the throat. Several open making a fine spike. A fine midseason pink. Should become a good commercial.

PASADENA. (D) Orange scarlet throat and lip white with purplish specks in the throat. Very large wavy flowers. Several open. Very showy.

PAULINE KUNDERD. (K) Light rose pink with creamy throat. Tall plant with several blooms open at a time. Very fine but rather slow propagator.

PAUL PFITZER. (Pf.) Very beautiful reddish purple, the finest in just this color. Something like Purple Glory but clearer, more brilliant coloring. Tall, strong plant.

PEACE. (Gropf) An old white variety with purplish spot in the throat. Tall strong plant. Still a good commercial late white.

PEARL OF CALIFORNIA. (Kingsley) Very large La France pink. Tall strong growing plant with 2 or 3 long side shoots. 8-12 blooms open. Early. An outstanding variety that should become a fine commercial.

PERSIA. Very deep red, almost black. Exceedingly popular. Always in good demand.

PFITZER'S FORTUNA. (Pf.) Large soft clear yellow. Many open. Early.

PFITZER'S TRIUMPH. (Pf.) Brilliant salmon with deep salmon red blotch. Immense blooms. Very beautiful and distinctive. One of the very finest.

PHAENOMEN. (Pf.) Soft salmon pink with clear yellow lip. Several open. Early. Rather short plant but beautiful ruffled variety.

PHILATELIA. (K) Deep tyrian rose feathered darker. Tall, strong plant. Very good.

PHILIP BREITMEYER. (K) Light rose lavender. Dark lines in the throat.

PINK CLOUD. (K) Large ruffled delicate rose shading to deeper rose throat. Several open. Distinctive and pretty.

PINK DELIGHT. (K) Soft rich rose pink. Cream throat.

PINK ENCHANTOR. (K) Rich rose pink with deep rose red blotch.

PINK LILY. (K) Very pretty ruffled deep rose pink.

POMPEIAN BEAUTY. (K) Deep rose pink with throat markings of red and white.

POND LILY. (K) Large deep rose pink, deeper in throat. Beautiful.

PRESIDENT HARDING. (White) Deep yet soft American Beauty color. Heavily ruffled. 8-10 open. This is somwehat like Diener's American Beauty but much better. I think you will like it.

PRESIDENT LINCOLN. (K) Lavender blue flaked darker, purple blotch on lower petals. Tall. This looks good.

PRETTY PINK. (K) Rose pink with deeper colored throat.

PRIDE OF OREGON. (Damon) Light pink. Large showy spike with many open. Fine.

PRIDE OF PORTLAND. (Ellis) Very large light rose. Winner of A. G. S. Trophy for best new seedling at the Northwest Regional Show.

PRIDE OF WANAKAH. (Criswell) Large beautiful lavender rose. Rich color, fine. You will like it.

PRIMROSE PRINCESS. (Salbach) Tall clear primrose yellow, lower petals darker. Long spikes of well placed blooms. Several open. Strong grower. One of the best light yellows.

PRINCE OF INDIA. (CHILDS) An old smoky variety that is always in demand.

PUREST OF ALL. (PF.) Large pure white with no markings. Many open· One of the best whites.

PURPLE GLORY. (K) Tall, strong growing plant with massive deep velvety maroon flowers with almost black blotches. Heavily ruffled. One of the best. Well liked by everyone.

PURPLE PROGRESS. (K) About the same color as Baron Hulot but much larger and better.

PURPLE QUEEN. (K) Deep violet purple. Several large well placed ruffled blooms open at a time. The best in this shade.

QUEEN MARY. (SALBACH) Bright ruffled pink with scarlet blotch on yellow ground of lower petals. Fine substance.

QUINTON. (KEMP) Very large light pink shading a little darker toward the edges of the petals. Pink lines on light yellow lip. Tall slender willowy stems that are fine for florist work. Very early and an easy grower.

RADIANT ORANGE. (AUSTIN) Large clear apricot orange. Always noticed in the garden. Good.

RADIANT QUEEN. (HORNBERGER) Fine orange P. G.

RAVENNA. (K) Dark purplish red. Long spike. One of Kunderd's best.

REAH. (SALBACH) An unusual shade called mallow purple shading to mallow pink. Very dark blotch in throat. Whole flower has a velvety appearance. Fine and distinct. Everyone likes it.

RED FIRE. (K) Large clear bright red. Long spike with several open. One of the best.

RED GLORY. (PIPER) A sport of Purple Glory. Beautiful dark red.

RED SPLENDOR. (K) Light scarlet, lower petals darker. Ruffled. Very strong and massive and stands winds and weather well. A good one.

RED TORNADO. (ELLIS) Heavy textured velvety red with darker throat.

RED VELVET. (K) Deep velvety cardinal red flaked darker. Very pretty.

REFLECTION. (GOODRICH) White. Upper petals tinged grenadine pink which appears as a reflection of the scarlet blotches on lower petals.

REMARKABLE. (K) Deep cherry rose. Large round flowers. Tall strong plant. Much admired by garden visitors.

RENOWN. (ERREY) Cream white, many blooms open. Tall and strong. Good.

RESPLENDENT. (KINYON) An odd but pretty combination of cream, yellow and scarlet. Heavily ruffled. Very showy.

REV. EWBANK. (VELTHUYS) Light blue. Several open. Tall but often kinked spikes. Early. Fine commercial and good seller.

RICHARD DIENER. (DIENER) Beautiful salmon pink, cream throat. Rather short plant but long spike with 8-10 blooms open. A fine variety either for the garden or as a commercial. Late.

RIPPLING WATERS. (ELLIS) Cream suffused with pink. Several large well placed blooms open. Fine.

RITA BECK. (FISCHER) Clear shell pink with scarlet lines on the lip. 6-8 immense blooms open. Tall straight stem that always stands up well in spite of the large flowers. An outstanding variety either for the garden or for florist use.

R. J. KUNDERD. (K) Wonderful dazzling orange vermillion. Several open. Fine.

RODERICK DHU. (STEPHEN) Rose pink sport of Mrs. Pendleton. Extremely large and beautiful color. Very showy.

ROMANCE. (K) Salmon rose bordered blue. Odd but very pretty. Fine spike with many open. One of the best.

ROSE ASH. (DIENER) A pastel shade. Ashes of roses. One of the best smokies. Tall. Popular.

ROSE MULBERRY. (AUSTIN) The name describes it. Tall plant. Several blooms open. A very pretty smoky.

19

A. B. Kunderd

Mrs. Hornberger

Ruffled Gold

20

Rita Beck

Rose Mist

Pres. Harding

ROYAL LAVENDER. (SCHLEIDER) Deep lavender shading lighter towaed the center. Heavy penciling of a deeper shade on lower petals 4 ft. high 14-20 buds,. 4-7 large flowers open at a time. A warm distinct shade that appeals to everyone.

This variety was originated by John Schleider of Michigan and grown for him for several years by Henry Winklehaus a florist of Howell. Mich. Mr. Winklehaus considers it the finest glad he ever grew. He says it is a wonderful seller in his store.

This past year Mr. Winklehaus grew some to exhibit at the Michigan Show. He brought. 21 spikes, the first 21 to bloom. They were magnificent. They had 4 ft. stems tho' I will admit they were cut rather low. The picture below is taken from a snapshot photograph of the basket. I grew just as good ones here on my poor sand but they were not quite so tall.

Royal Lavender is a very fine variety for any purpose but its greatest value will be as a commercial flower. If I know anything about glads it will become a leading commercial lavender in a few years. Another thing about this variety is that old bulbs do .not deteriorate. With most varieties when a bulb gets 3 or 4 years old it peters out and is no good but Royal Lavender keeps right on year after year producing flne spikes of bloom and nice plump bulbs tho of course not so many bulblets. I do not fill orders with these old bulbs but am just telling how they act.

If you have any doubt about the value of this variety, write Henry Winklehaus, Howell, Mich. He has grown more of them and used more in floral work than anyone else. You can't go wrong on Royal Lavender.

*Basket Shown
at the
Michigan
Show at
Lansing, 1929*

ROYAL PURPLE. (K) Beautiful large violet purple.

RUDOLPH VALENTINO. (VELTHUYS) Bright pink of fine substance. Stands weather well.

RUFFLED GOLD. (GOODRICH) Beautifully and heavily ruffled light yellow with rose pink feather in throat. 6-8 perfectly placed blooms open. Slender but stiff stem. Tall. Very artistic and beautiful yellow that is different.

SACAJAWEA OR SMOKY. (D) Golden bronze, a pretty distinct new shade. Tall. Strong grower.

ST. THOMAS. (K) Large salmon rose tinged with scarlet with a deep purplish black blotch. Very showy. Attracts lots of attention in the garden.

SALBACH'S PINK. (SALBACH) Large wide open geranium pink with soft carmine lip and throat. Long spike with 6-8 large flowers open. Opens well to the end.

SARABAND. (SALBACH) Rich velvety bordeaux or deep mulberry, straw yellow blotch. Very unusual and beautiful color. Large flowers. Fine.

SCARLET KING. (K) Large bright scarlet.

SCARLET PRINCEPS. (K) An old but very good bright red. A big seller everywhere.

SCARLET WONDER. (GROFF) Immense clear red. The largest red grown, often 6 inches across. Extremely showy in the garden.

SENORITA. (SALBACH) Large, wide open orange shading to salmon. Red pencilings on bright orange yellow lower petals. Many open. Extremely showy. Medium height,

SIDNEY PLUMMER. (SALBACH) Large cream yellow tinged delicate pink, amber lip marked with purplish lines. 8 or more well placed blooms open. Blooms from any size bulb. No. 3 will give magnificent spikes. A fine variety for any purpose.

Pearl of California

SIR THOMAS LIPTON. (SALBACH) Large salmon rose flaked with steel. Attractive. Strong grower.

SMOKE. (DIENER) Old rose streaked with slaty pink. Odd but always attracts attention in the garden. Never have enough to go around.

STAR OF THE SEA. (ELLIS) Large reddish orange. Looks somewhat like Mrs. Leon Douglas except in color.

STUTTGARDIA. (PFITZER) Bright orange which fades some in the sun. Except for this it would be a fine variety.

SULPHUR FRILLS. (K) Heavily ruffled clear sulphur yellow. Very popular.

SULTAN. (Crow) Very deep red, heavily ruffled. A seedling of Purple Glory and Dr. Bennett. Many blooms open. Beautiful velvety texture. A fine exhibition variety. One of the best.

SWEET ROSE. (K) Soft deep rose pink with red throat. Large, beautiful pink.

SWORD OF MAHOMET. (Ellis) A smoky brown, very pretty. Tall, strong grower. One of the best smokies.

TARO. (K) Cerise, darker than American Beauty. Early. Massive grower. Fine commercial variety.

THAIS VALDEMAR. (Diener) Old rose, overlaid with bright vermillion. General appearance is a self color. Very pretty.

THE PRESIDENT. (K) Light red. Well liked by garden visitors.

THISTLE. (K) Ruffled dark salmon pink with darker markings. Distinctive and very pretty.

THOS. T. KENT. (Diener) Light shell pink overlaid with strawberry red. Crimson stripe on each petal. 9 or more very large blooms open at a time making a very showy spike. Not beautiful but showy.

THOMAS A. EDISON. (K) Very heavily ruffled very deep red. Velvety texture. The finest in just this shade.

TIGER. (K) An odd but very well liked color. Salmon red flaking on outer portion of petals. Large smoky blue blotch bordered white.

TITAN. (Errey) Very large salmon pink with purplish blotch. Nice color. Several open. Attracts lots of attention in the garden.

TOBERSUN. (Austin) Large clear yellow. A little lighter shade than Loyalty but very good. Several open. Tall, strong plant. One of the best yellows.

TROUBADOUR. (Pfitzer) Large clear purple. Long spike with many well placed blooms open. A fine one.

TWILIGHT. (K) Very beautiful ruffled creamy buff with yellow and pink throat. Strong heavy foilage. Fine.

TYCKO ZANG. (Austin) Immense salmon pink, white throat faintly dotted cerise. Several open. Very large heavy foilage. Tall, strong grower and good propagator.

VEILCHENBLAU. (Pfitzer) Large dark blue. The best on the market in this shade.

VEILED BRILLIANCE. (Austin) Bright pink tinted grayish giving it the appearance of being veiled. Several large well placed blooms open. Tall strong plant. One of my favorites. Fine.

VELVET DIAMOND. (K) Rich velvety blood red.

VIOLET PRINCE. (K) Very deep reddish violet.

WABAN. (Stephen) Bright orange with darker blotch. Very showy and pretty. You will like it.

WAWASEE. (K) Soft rose pink striped bright rose or red. Red blotch in throat. Showy and always well liked by garden visitors.

WEDGEWOOD. (Austin) Strong growing violet purple. Fine.

W. H. PHIPPS. (Diener) A real wonder gladiolus. Light rose salmon. 15-20 or more large wide open blooms open at a time. When well grown this is about the ultimate as an exhibition flower. Is becoming well known as a commercial too.

W. G. BADGER. (Metzner) Light salmon. Throat cream dotted with cerise. Nearly whole spike open at a time,

WODAN. (Pfitzer) Deep violet blue. Fine. Clear color. Medium height.

YELLOW PERFECTION. (Pfitzer) Clear light yellow. Many blooms open at a time.

PRIMULINUS VARIETIES.

This class of glads is different from the others in having usually a more slender stem, flowers farther apart on the stem, often smaller flowers tho not always, a greater range of color especially the orange and yellow and pastel shades and delicate colors and sometimes the blooms are hooded tho the later originations do not usually show this so much. They are strong growers and good propagators. They have a more artistic form and are especially fine in baskets and artistic floral work.

You should try some. You will like them.

ADA DE POY. (SALBACH) Clear apricot with bronze shadings. Long spikes with 6-8 blooms open. Ruffled. Very artistic and pretty.

AFLAME. (HORNBERGER) Begonia rose shading to bright orange flame near the edge. Back of petals is even brighter than the front. Very large. 6 inches and over across. One customer wrote me that he didn't suppose a glad could grow so big. 6 or more open. A very fine variety.

APRICOT GLOW. (PALMER) Clear, warm apricot shade fading a little as it stands but still a beautiful color. Very seldom flecks as do most varieties. The color is very similar to Gloriana but it is better in every other way. Gloriana is a very beautiful glad but is surpassed by Apricot Glow. It has the strong growth and nearly the size of Giant Nymph but the grace and beauty of the finest prim. Easily grows 5-5½ ft. high and can be cut with a fine stem without sacrificing the plant and bulb.

This past summer I sent some blooms to several of the leading florists of Boston and N. Y. solely with the idea of getting their opinions of Apricot Glow as a commercial flower. Nearly all were enthusiastic about it and several wanted to buy flowers and this at a time when the market was flooded with glads. We shipped blooms as long as they lasted and got several times the regular market price.

The following letter from Max Schling probably the best known retail florist in America is typical of several I received from the florists I sent blooms to.

"Among the many varieties of similar types, Apricot Glow is without question one of the finest in form, color and size of flowers. I have among my collection some of the best produced in Europe and in our own United States and, with the exception of Orange Queen, I have not come across one that has such fine nuanciation in coloring.

I regret that I was absent from the city at the first meeting of the New York Florist's Club and was for the two weeks previous not in touch with any of our own people, otherwise I would have tried to get to them the message somehow to ask you to send some of these gladiolus to be exhibited at the New York Florist's Club. I am quite sure if you would send some of these stalks next year of the same type, to be judged by the exhibition committee of the New York Florist's Club it will do you no harm. The Horticultural Society of Massachusetts has a similar committee and it would be perhaps worthwhile to send some there. Get in contact with Mr. E. I. Farrington at the Horticultural Hall in Boston.

The flowers themselves lasted, regardless of the exceedingly warm season, eleven days after having traveled from Burlington to New York and on arrival in New York having been shipped to me, which took another day. Almost every bud developed perfectly."

I really believe this is one of the finest florist varieties ever introduced and will be grown by the million. It is a fine propagator.

CARA MIA. (MILLER) Deep shrimp pink with small light rose spot on lower petals. Tall slender but stiff stems. This is the earliest variety I have ever grown. Being so extremely early and fine in other respects it should become a valuable commercial variety.

COPPER BRONZE. (K) Very large coppery bronze. One of the most distinctively beautiful and artistic primulinus in existence.

COPPER GOLD. (K) A beautiful gold tinged with copper. Tall strong grower.

E. B. WILLIAMSON. (K) Light purple, a new shade in prims. If you like purple shades you will like this.

ENCHANTRESS. (K) Large beautiful soft shrimp pink.

Apricot Glow

26

ETHELYN. (FISCHER) Tall straight orange similar to Orange Queen but has a clear lip instead of deep orange lines on it. Has side shoots that make good long stems. One of the very finest prims in existence.

EVENING. (K) Very dainty flesh pink with cream throat.

FIRY KNIGHT. (HOFMAN) Large clear fiery red. Fine.

GOLDEN FRILLS. (K) Tall heavily ruffled very deep yellow. Small flame cerise feather in the throat which deepens the general color. Very artistic and beautiful. One of Kunderds' best.

GOLDEN ORANGE. (K) Beautiful golden orange color.

GOLDIELOCKS. (STEPHEN) Beautiful pure clear soft yellow. Frank Shepardson, President of the A. G. S. a man who knows his glads says "Chaste" is the word that describes it.

HARBINGER. (SANFORD) Burnt orange, different from any other shade known in gladiolus. This is as fine a variety for landscape use as I ever saw. Better try a few.

IMPROVED TIPLADY. (SALBACH) Orange, little darker than Tiplady and taller, not quite so large a flower.

KING OF ORANGES. (K) Large orange saffron. Good.

KUNDERDS' YELLOW BEAUTY. (K) A good yellow.

MARIGOLD. (K) Large ruffled light yellow.

MONGOLIA. (K) Very deep yellow, probably the deepest yellow glad to date. Clear self color. Tall plants. Good sized flower. Good.

MRS. CALVIN COOLIDGE. (K) Large soft salmon rose, cream toward center. Ruffled. One of the very best.

ONETA. (KEMP) Orange. Very tall strong growing plant. Large flower of fine color. One of the best orange glads on the market. Should be better known.

ORANGE BUTTERFLY. (SALBACH) Bright bronzy orange of fine substance. Several well arranged flowers of butterfly shape. A spike of blooms looks like a flock of butterflies in flight. Distinctive and very pretty.

ORANGE QUEEN. (HOLLAND) Beautiful light orange, deeper at edge of petals. Orange red lines in the throat. Tall, 5-7 blooms open. One of the very best commercial glads and one of the big sellers.

PANSY. (K) Salmon red with velvety orange red blotches. Tall, early. This does not seem to be well known but is one of the finest prims.

PATRICIA CARTER. (K) Soft clear light shrimp pink. Very dainty and beautiful.

QUEEN OF ORANGE. (K) Immense orange red. 5 inches across, Very showy.

ROSE MIST. (FISCHER) A prim in a class by itself. The color is difficult to describe. It is a sort of old rose with buff showing thro. Fine buff line on edge of all petals. 5-6 or more well placed blooms on tall spike. One of the most beautiful of all glads.

SALMON GLOW. (HORNBERGER) Very large beautiful clear salmon, clear yellow lip. 5 inches or more across. Extremely early and valuable commercially for that reason.

SCARLET BEDDER. (SALBACH) Beautiful soft yet glowing scarlet. Very distinctive and beautiful. Sure to be popular.

SWEETER SEVENTEEN. (K) Large clear deep salmon pink, yellow throat.

TAURUS. (K) Distinct shade of purple violet. Good seller.

TEMBLOR. (K) Large clear dark salmon, cream throat. Very good.

THE ORCHID. (SPRAGUE) Orchid shape and color. Badly hooded but very pretty.

WINIFRED. (STEPHEN) Peculiar combination of purplish plum and yellow. Very long spike with 10-12 open at a time. Very odd and distinctive. A good one.

VIRGINIA LOU. (K) Old rose, creamy yellow throat. Large and fine.

ZONA. (K) Deep salmon rose on upper petals. Lower petals lighter with a fiery rose blotch on yellow ground. Very beautiful. Tall strong grower.

Delphiniums

Delphiniums are positively the best blue hardy perennial. They grow to nine feet and taller, and with their long, stately spikes of flowers and broad leaves they are in a class by themselves. They grow well in any good, well-cultivated garden soil, are absolutely hardy, produce bloom twice during the season and will give more garden pleasure than any perennial I know.

Blooms from Seedling Plants

There has been a great revival of interest in Delphiniums the past few years due to the wonderful inprovements that have been made in them. Several famous hybridizers have been working on them and have produced new forms and types and wonderfully beautiful colorings, many of them now having beautiful shades of pink, mauve and purple mingled with the various shades of blue.

I no longer grow the old common strains but am offering year-old plants of the Vanderbilt strain which is considered as fine as there is in existence. I get the very finest seed to be had, the same as the originators use for their own sowing.

In August, 1926, I exhibited blooms from seedling plants at the Boston Gladiolus Show and at two or three other flower shows and at every show the people went wild over them. One lady told me she had paid high prices for named varieties that could not compare with mine.

28

They can be planted either in the fall or spring but if in the spring you should order them during the winter so I can ship just as soon as the frost is out of the ground.

One year old plants, strong sturdy plants with unusual root growth, $4.00 per dozen, prepaid.

BABY SEEDLINGS. These plants look small when you get them but they will bloom this first year. They will bloom later however than the large plants and do not all bloom at the same time as do the large ones but the blooming season extends throughout the summer. A good way is to get both large plants and seedlings and so extend the blooming season of your delphiniums. Baby Seedlings $1.50 per dozen, postpaid.

Apricot Glow

Phlox

One of the very best and showiest hardy plants. This year I have them only by color: white, light pink, salmon pink and lavender or purple. They are fine varieties $2.00 per dozen, prepaid.

One of our Fields, 1929

Montbretias

These are very pretty bright-colored summer-flowering bulbs. Somewhat like a very small-flowered gladiolus. The slender wiry stems grow about two feet high or higher, and have the flowers arranged about one-third the length. Very artistic and beautiful. They should be planted in clumps for best effect. In mild climates they can be left in the ground two or three years with a winter cover. Mixed orange and red, 50 cents a dozen; $3.50 per 100. Better try at least one dozen.

A DELIGHTFUL LITTLE BOOK
"GOD'S LOVELIEST CREATIONS—A CHILD AND A FLOWER"

Sixty-eight pages of beautiful tributes in poetry and prose paid to mothers, to children and to flowers by eminent people of the past and present time. Here are three specimen tributes:

> "Mothers and flowers to men were given,
> To bridge the span twixt earth and Heaven,'"

> "There is no joy like that which surrounds a cradle."

"Flowers are the sweetest things that God ever made and forgot to put a soul into."
A splendid gift to Mothers any day, with or without flowers. A copy should be in every home blessed with children or flower-lovers. **Fifty Cents per Copy** Copyright, 1929, by Charles A. Robinson, 597 Parke Avenue, East Orange, New Jersey.
Send direct to Mr. Robinson. I get nothing for this, just want to pass along a good thing.

JOIN THE AMERICAN GLADIOLUS SOCIETY, the fastest growing special flower society in the world. Dues $2.00 a year. You receive a monthly magazine devoted solely to the gladiolus. It contains a world of valuable information for glad lovers. Worth much more than the $2.00.

To all new members I will send a bulb of Copper Bronze and Golden Frills. This is not for transfers but to bonafide new members.

If You are a Member Please Hand this to Some Friend

"I hereby apply for membership in the American Gladiolus Society, and inclose $2.00 as annual membership dues, $1.00 of which is for a year's subscription to the Gladiolus Review.

Mail this application and $2.00 to
ROSCOE HUFF, Secretary
Goshen, Indiana

Name...

Street and No...

City or Town...State...

Amateur or Professional...
Recommended by Elmer E. Gove.

THE NEW ENGLAND GLADIOLUS SOCIETY, is another big glad society that is doing big things. They issue a very fine illustrated year book of nearly 100 pages that is worth more than the yearly dues. New members coming in this year will get copies of both the 1929 and 1930 year books. Dues $1.00 a year.

Please enroll me as a member of the
NEW ENGLAND GLADIOLUS SOCIETY
Mail this coupon and $1.00 to
C. W. BROWN, Secretary
Ashland, Mass.

Name...

Street...

P. O..State...
Recommended by Elmer E. Gove.

TESTIMONIALS

"I have just received set No. 79, Orange Queen and I hasten to say that it surpasses all expectations. I thank you cordially for your superior stock and I certainly will be with you with my orders for next spring, for my requirements in varieties you offer. I am taking over this entire set to the next meeting of our Horticultural society in order to let them see a fine example of perfect gladiolus stock." F. E. B., Toronto, Can.

"Just wish to acknowledge safe receipt several days ago of the glads you sent me—certainly wish to thank you for your kindness and generosity in count, and to tell you that your bulbs have been the nicest and cleanest that I have had from anywhere this season. I have had several orders from you and all have been uniformly very good. Mrs. A. A. C., Kansas City,Kan

'Just a line to say that the gladiolus bulbs purchased from you this last spring are now in full bloom and the most beautiful assortment that I have ever purchased. Words can hardly express my thanks to you for these flowers have brought at least 50 visitors to my home the past week and everyone has said that they never saw their equal in any flower garden. Every plant is strong, everyone standing upright and I have plants from 4 to 5 feet high." W. J. McKee, Oconomowoc, Wis.

"Just a few lines to let you know that I and my family have had a world of pleasure from the blooms your glad bulbs have produced. They have all been wonderful and especially do I wish to thank you for the extras you sent me. Gloriana, Marnia and Lorice have been just beautiful and among the best in my whole garden." Mrs. L. B. F., Chillicothe, Ohio.

"Thought I would write you about my success with my glads this season. Won silver cup for winning the most firsts. Copper Bronze took well, everyone seemed to just rave over it." John. J. R., Meadville, Pa.

"Bought a couple of hundred of your bulbs last spring and was mighty well pleased. Want to order more. C. B. W., West Monroe, N. Y.

"Am pleased to say the set you sent me during summer turned out splendidly. All bloomed. Golden Dream overdid itself by giving me 4 bulbs 2 inches in diameter and 14 bulblets 3-8 to ½ inch besides numerous small ones. The delphinium roots were the finest I have seen.
E. V. W., Birmingham, Ala.

"I received your shipment of bulbs for which I express my appreciation. The order was only for a dollar but in all my experience of buying I have never received such prompt and courteous service and above all such wonderful value in comparison with other gladiolus dealers. My only regret is that I did not give you my entire gladiolus order this year."
C. J. L., Woodhaven, L. I., N. Y.

Below are some books that everyone having a garden should own. I can take your order and have them sent direct from the publisher.

Farm and Garden Rule Book, by **L**. H. Bailey. **A** reference book with a fund of useful knowledge for every farm and garden enterprise, presented in easily located rules, recipes, formulae, and tables. Ill., 587 pp. **$3.00**

My Garden Comes of Age, by Julia H. Cummins. An account of the evolution of a deserted farmstead into a charming home. The author recounts her trials and successes in rebuilding and refurnishing the old house and in developing the garden. Ill., 180 pp. **$3.00**

Around the Year in the Garden, by F. F. Rockwell. Because the time when you do your garden work is so important, you need a regular schedule. This book gives you complete information on every garden problem, outlined week by week, and written by a practical gardener. 88 Ill., 350 pp. **$3.50**

The Gardener, by **L**. H. Bailey. You get full advantage of Dr. Bailey's un-equalled knowledge and experience in this book. It tells how to grow flowers, vegetables, and fruits from time of planting through to maturity. Special articles on different types of gardening. Information that is easy to find and simple to use. 116 Ill., 260 pp. **$2.00**

Home Flower Growing, by E. C. Volz. A real flower garden encyclopedia! It, will teach you how to propagate and cultivate your plants, how to care for, fertilize and maintain them. It tells how and when and where to grow flowers; what different kinds look alike; how to plan indoor, outdoor, rock, and water gardens; how to prepare exhibits for a flower show; how to organize a garden club. 151 Ill., 364 pp. **$3.50**

Lawns, by F. F. Rockwell. You will find use for this information year after year, for it shows both how to start a lawn right and how to keep it smooth and velvety thereafter. Full of suggestions on laying out the lawn, grading, fertilizing, planting, care after planting, weed and pest control, and remaking and repairing old lawns. 39 Ill., 87 pp. **$1.00**

Manual of Gardening, by **L**. H. Bailey. You can depend on this book to supply you with complete and practical information on planting and landscaping your home grounds. Tells how to make the most of natural features; how to drain, cultivate, and fertilize the soil; how to sow, propagate, transplant, prune, and graft the different varieties of fruits, vegetables, and flowers. Gives lists of varieties suited for different purposes. 350 Ill., 539 pp. **$3.00**

Rock Gardens, by F. F. Rockwell. Shows just how you can build a rock garden yourself, on a small or large scale and at little expense. Describes the types of rock gardens, tells what soils, climates, and locations are best, how to construct, and what to plant for the effect you want. 31 Ill., 86 pp. **$1.00**

THE GLADIOLUS BOOK
is about the most complete treatise published on the gladiolus. Is written by Forman T. McLean, William Edwin Clark and Eugene H. Fischer; 224 pages finely bound and worthy of a place in any library. Price, $5 plus 10 cents for postage. If you are a real "glad bug" you want this book.